YOUR FUTURE IN MUSIC

YOUR FUTURE
IN
MUSIC

Robert E. Curtis

RICHARDS ROSEN PRESS, INC.
New York, New York 10010

Published in 1962, 1976 by Richards Rosen Press, Inc.
29 East 21st Street, New York, N.Y. 10010

Copyright 1962, 1976 by Robert E. Curtis

SECOND EDITION

Library of Congress Cataloging in Publication Data

Curtis, Robert E
  Your future in music.

  1. Music as a profession. I. Title.
ML3795.C87 1976   780′.23   75–28428
ISBN 0–8239–0354–0

Manufactured in the United States of America

About the Author

From living out of suitcases on one-night stands with Artie Shaw's Orchestra to midnight sessions on Madison Avenue to programming and arranging music material for the Pat Boone show, Robert E. Curtis has ranged over the entire field of popular music.

Born in Boston, the son of a doctor, young Curtis vetoed the idea of following in his father's footsteps, but he did follow them as far as Harvard, where he had the great good fortune to study with Walter Piston. By this time, the young student had already had considerable musical training—piano lessons from the age of five, violin lessons soon thereafter, and instruction on the saxophone and clarinet a little later. After college, he traveled with such big-name orchestras as Artie Shaw, Tommy Dorsey, Gene Krupa, and Red Norvo.

Mr. Curtis has worked extensively as an arranger, composer, conductor, and pianist, and in the course of his career has been closely associated with such personalities as Frank Sinatra, Percy Faith, Raymond Scott, Dorothy Collins, and Pat Boone.

At his home—known as "The Garden of Weedin' "—on Long Island's north shore, Mr. Curtis's chief domestic problem is persuading his teen-age son and daughter to perform the gardening chores, which, according to Mrs. Curtis, are the solemn obligation of the man of the house. When not thus occupied, he commutes to a plush Manhattan office, where, in a quiet corner, he composes and orchestrates jingles that Madison Avenue uses to whet consumer appetites.

Contents

Introduction

Come join me in the fascinating world of music, but only if you are ambitious and studious, have a strong heart and stomach, and can take the bad with the good. In this glamorous but lopsided field you will meet and intimately know celebrities and nonentities, geniuses and dullards, freethinkers and conventionalists, extroverts and introverts, music lovers and music haters, as well as hosts of just ordinary people. You may not love them all, but before too many years have passed you should have a storehouse of interesting tales to tell your children.

People in music enjoy a freedom completely unknown to the organization man. (Unfortunately, this may also include, as former Secretary of Defense Wilson so inopportunely put it, "the freedom not to work.") The nine-to-five day is almost wholly foreign to the life of a musician, and he usually can avoid getting caught up in rush-hour traffic either going to work or coming home, if not both ways. As a composer he can give expression to the wildest flights of his imagination, even if he can't always be certain that he will hear his creations performed. As a teacher, although he must adhere to his schedule, he may exercise some choice over which hours and days he will teach and which he will not.

On the other hand, most musicians have to work when others are enjoying time off from their own labors, and this means nights, weekends, and holidays. And when arrangers and composers, whose assignments frequently come at the last minute, have deadlines to meet, they must necessarily work unceasingly and without regard to the clock until those assignments are completed. Besides, starting times of most jobs are rigidly enforced. You just don't come in late to a concert, a Broadway musical, or a television show.

Few other fields offer such a mixture of exciting, talented people, such freedom, or such diversity of opportunity for making a living. Few other fields offer such chances for fame and fortune and few other fields bring to so many of their older members such bitter disillusionment.

Yes, come join me in the wonderful world of music. If you had been in the field in the mid-1970's, you might have been British-born singer Elton John. A superstar by 1974, all 75,000 tickets for his four performances in Inglewood, California were sold out in a matter of hours after going on sale. You might be Russian cellist Mstislav Rostopovich, playing to standing ovations on his two year American tour after which he may not be permitted to return to Russia. If you were black or a woman, the music world would be more open to you than a decade ago. In mass music, particularly, black artists have been very popular. You might be Grammy award winners Roberta Flack, Gladys Knight or Stevie Wonder, the pop vocalist who won four Grammy Awards in 1973. You could be Leonard Bernstein who, after achieving a world-wide reputation as a conductor (and frequent piano soloist) of the N.Y. Philharmonic, composer of serious and Broadway scores, was appointed an institute lecturer at M.I.T. If you were Donald Martino, you would have received the 1974 Pulitzer Prize for your largely twelve tone compositions. You could be Daniel Barenboim who, after a successful career as a pianist, turned to conducting as well and took over the direction of the Orchestra de Paris in the fall of 1975. You could be Mahavishnu John McLaughlin who formed his own orchestra after being a Miles Davis sideman credited with 1974's jazz revival in which jazz records hit the charts and stayed there. You might be keyboard artist Herbie Hancock or trumpeter Donald Byrd, both of whom received gold records for album sales in excess of $1 million. You could be singer Barbra Streisand, one of the nation's top box-office draws, who has made six TV specials, eleven albums and numerous movies. You might be Beverly Sills, operatic superstar, soprano with the N.Y. City Opera for twenty years, who made her Metropolitan Opera debut at the age of forty-six. She is perhaps the highest paid opera singer in the world, receiving as much as $10,000 for a single opera performance and even more for a recital. You might be twenty-four year old Eugene Fodor of Colorado who, in 1974, shared second prize with two Soviet violinists at the Tchaikovsky competition in Moscow and returned to the U.S. to play for President and Mrs. Ford at the White House. You might have been a youngster trying to get started, willing to play anywhere for any money just to get his break; or you might have been an oldster whose work and savings began to evaporate just when he needed them most to send his children through college. It can be exciting and it can be lucrative. It can be wonderful because you can develop your own talents and observe your own progress toward acquiring riches and achieving recognition. But if these are your ambitions and they go unfulfilled, heartache and disappointment may be yours.

In this and the following chapters I shall attempt to point up the numerous opportunities that exist for qualified aspirants in the field of music. I shall examine a number of specific jobs in detail, outlining the demands made upon individuals so employed and stressing the qualities that help lead to success in these efforts. Also I shall report the financial returns to be expected from different kinds of positions. Along with this, I'll try to enumerate the pitfalls and the hazards that may be encountered.

I shall attempt, insofar as possible, to treat separately the three main classifications—playing, writing (arranging and composing), and teaching. I shall set forth the vast rewards that have accrued to various gifted individuals, thereby demonstrating the almost limitless possibilities that exist in the field; but I shall show the appalling amount of unemployment that has plagued this occupation for many years.

But first let us survey the field and see what the opportunities are and where they exist.

Masculine pronouns are being used for succinctness and are intended to refer to both females and males.

YOUR FUTURE IN MUSIC

CHAPTER I

Survey

As previously stated, careers in music are neatly divided into three classifications—performing, writing, and teaching. But there the neatness ends. When a man tells you that he is a musician, he has given you nothing but the vaguest notion of what he does for a living. Does he play or conduct? Does he arrange or compose? Perhaps he teaches, or possibly he earns his living by working in two or even all three categories. But what precisely does he do? For what specific kind of work does his training and experience prepare him? And with what kinds of music is he involved?

If he performs for a living and is not a conductor, which instrument or instruments does he play? If he earns a fairly steady living, the chances are that he plays one or more of the most common orchestral instruments. He may play one of the string group such as violin, viola, 'cello, or string bass, and the fact that there is today an increasing shortage of good string players may be worth noting. He may play one or more of the wood-wind group—flute, oboe, English horn, clarinet, bassoon, bass clarinet, or contra-bassoon. It is to be remarked that playing the bass clarinet is generally the function of the clarinetist and that the contra-bassoon is played by the bassoonist. And while English horn playing is indeed a specialty, in the symphony orchestra the English horn player may be called upon to play the third or fourth oboe part (on oboe), and in studio orchestras the oboist is almost invariably called upon to play English horn. To proceed, he may play French horn or any of the instruments of the brass group, trumpet or cornet, trombone or bass trombone, or tuba. If percussion is our man's domain, he probably plays all of the percussion instruments, which include kettledrums, snare drum, bass drum, cymbals, triangle, tambourine, glockenspiel, wood block, tam-tam, xylophone, vibraphone, bells and chimes, as well as a host of other related instruments, or, in the symphony orchestra, he may confine his activities solely to one of the percussion categories. He may play harp or guitar or any of the keyboard family such as piano, organ, accordion, or even harpsichord, which has enjoyed a revival in the last thirty years. One instrument that our man may play, especially if his work lies in the field of dance orchestras, dance bands, or jazz groups, is saxophone.

Most other instruments are employed so infrequently as to be unable to provide a primary source of income, but the more rarely used instruments do provide an excellent source of additional income when played as secondary instruments. However, I know of several cases of harmonica players, for example, whose services are in constant demand because of the extraordinary level of their artistry. Thus, while it is possible to pursue a successful career by playing one of the rarely used instruments, it seems a wiser course to strive for great proficiency on one of the more common instruments.

If a man is an instrumentalist, what are his job opportunities? Well, to determine what kind of work he may do, one must consider his training and experience. If his training has been strictly in the realm of concert or what is often called "serious" music, he would be best suited to working with a large symphony orchestra or with one or more smaller orchestral ensembles. Practically every large city in the U.S. has a large orchestra, and many cities have, in addition, smaller groups like string orchestras, various types of chamber groups such as wood-wind groups, brass ensembles, string quartets, as well as mixed chamber orchestras, sometimes independent of and sometimes in conjunction with Haydn, Bach, Handel, etc. societies.

Several South American cities maintain, to a degree, symphony and other types of orchestras. A few cities in the U.S. and in South America that have opera or ballet companies employ fair-sized orchestras, and the "legitimately" trained instrumentalist with good qualifications should fit into one of these orchestras.

However, most opera and ballet companies have notably short seasons.

In the largest cities in the U.S. where the legitimate theatre is active, serious musicians frequently find jobs in pit orchestras, but the tendency of the last few years, because of the increasing use of the jazz idiom in musical comedy scores, has been to use musicians with dance band backgrounds.

One exception to this trend is that of the string section. The best string writing is of a nature that is easily played well by legitimate string players. In fact, the best string writers have learned their lessons well by great familiarity with and imitation of the symphonic masters of the past and present. Another exception, and for the same reason as above, is that of the French horn player. Therefore, the string player and the French horn player with concert orchestra experience can fit into almost any type of situation—radio or TV orchestra, recording orchestra, pit band, stage band, concert jazz orchestra, night club or restaurant orchestra, etc. Concert and marching bands provide a limited amount of work for instrumentalists with *serious* training, but, of course, they don't employ any strings.

Some concert instrumentalists—largely string players and pianists —are soloists, and their livelihood is earned by giving solo recitals or by playing solo parts with orchestras. Their lives consist of practicing and traveling. These men are known as concert artists, although some reviewers have, on occasion, put this in question.

Concert pianists have a much wider range of activity than other serious instrumentalists. In addition to being concert soloists, they perform as members of the orchestra in many modern symphonies, in opera, and in the ballet as well as playing important parts in many chamber groups. Pianists work as accompanists to other instrumentalists and singers in recitals, they play alone for rehearsals of ballet and opera casts, and they even find employment in ballet schools. But the variety of opportunity for pianists is more than offset by the fact that in large orchestras, where one pianist (or sometimes two) is used only occasionally, some forty string players are regularly employed.

When we come to the field of popular, dance (in the popular dance band idiom), and jazz music, we have a great many more opportunities for work than there are for the so-called "serious" musician. But here we have cross relationships and other complicating factors. (For the sake of simplicity, I shall lump these three groups together and term their exponents "pop" musicians, except when I wish to be more specific, although, to be perfectly fair, most popular musicians could never hope to play in jazz groups.) In the first place, for instance, most musicians have learned their instruments by adhering to the strict discipline of legitimate training. They may not have carried their studies to completion, but, in most cases, they have carried them to the point where they have developed the basic resources that are common to the concert musician, especially as regards tone production, intonation, and technical facility. But by playing with dance bands, by listening to performances of other pop groups, and by orienting their playing in the direction of dance bands, they have learned to produce the sound and to play with the conception that so markedly distinguishes popular music from concert music playing; and, by so doing, they have become popular music specialists.

Others in the pop field, lacking in much formal training, are largely self-taught. The quality of their playing accurately reflects their tenacity and talent, their ingenuity and intelligence. Some of these performers are among the top musicians in the world; others display serious flaws and limitations when their playing is measured by the standards set for the better serious musicians. Some pop musicians are so versatile that they are equally at home in pop music or in concert. These men do the top free-lance work in New York, Chicago, and Los Angeles.

What instruments are used in pop music? The answer is that all of the common orchestral instruments are used, but there is a lot less call for some than for others. Not nearly so many strings are used in pop music as in concert music, and many, many groups use none at all. French horn is rarely used except in larger studio or recording orchestras. Harpists are generally limited to the same large studio and recording orchestras. Wood-wind players are almost never hired to play one instrument such as clarinet, oboe, or bassoon. They are almost always saxophone players who double on one or more of the wood-wind group. All saxophone players are required to be reasonably proficient on clarinet (or bass clarinet), but they need not play another wood-wind instrument except in certain specialized jobs or in studio work.

Pop musicians have a relatively large field that consists of such work as hotels, restaurants, night clubs, private dances, dance halls, stage bands, theatre orchestras, traveling groups or large bands or small "combos," jazz concerts, radio, TV, recording, transcription, film work, etc. Although many hotels, restaurants, and small clubs have switched over to taped music, numerous establishments throughout the country still use "live" music (but not nearly enough), and there seems to be a trend toward more live music. Nevertheless, despite the fact that the musician's union sets the minimum number of men allowed (whenever it can), the size of most groups remains quite small—usually three, four, or five men. Only the largest place can afford to have decent-sized orchestras, and even they, in an effort to keep expenses down, employ as few musicians as possible.

Instrumentation of pop groups varies with the whims of the leaders. There are virtually no standards today, but drums and string bass inevitably find their way into almost all groups. A trio might consist of piano, drums, and bass, or guitar, piano, and bass; a quartet might contain trumpet, baritone saxophone, drums, and bass; a sextet might consist of accordion, trumpet, saxophone, piano, drums, and bass. Regardless of the size of a group, there are almost as many combinations of instruments that can sound well as there are combinations of instruments. The traditional large studio orchestra consists of four trumpets, four trombones, five saxophones (two altos, two tenors, and one baritone, all of whom double on clarinet, one or more of whom plays oboe and English horn, one of whom doubles on bass clarinet, two or more of whom play flute, and one of whom plays bassoon), one harp, thirteen to fifteen or more strings (violins, violas, and 'celli), one piano, one guitar, one string bass, one drummer, one utility percussionist, and occasionally one tuba and from one to three French horns.

Pianists, accordionists, and organists enjoy the advantage of being able to play many kinds of solo engagements. Besides, pianists are employed extensively in the role of rehearsal pianists for shows of all sorts, whether for TV or stage. They even find a market for their services in the field of amateur theatricals. But the pianist has the advantage of still another market where he may do very well and make a name for himself—as pianist-arranger-conductor for a singer (preferably, of course, a big-name singer). And if he is neither arranger nor conductor, he can still be the singer's accompanist.

As for guitarists, they, too, can serve in the role of accompanists, arrangers, and conductors for singers, but pianists seem to get the nod in this department over almost any other instrumentalist. However, guitarists are enjoying a field day in recording, what with three and four guitars being used on every rock-and-roll date. Instrumentalists who play other instruments can, of course, conduct for singers and play in the instrumental background, but since instruments on which chords may be played are best suited to accompaniment, especially in the absence of an orchestra, men who play chord-producing instruments are usually chosen as conductor-accompanists.

We have seen from the above that in the field of accompaniment the musician is called upon to play the dual role of player and conductor. You have probably observed a number of orchestras where one of the players stood in front, and although he played solos and participated in the ensemble playing, it was obvious that he was the boss and was taking charge of things. It is because of this frequent overlapping of the roles of player and conductor that I have conveniently lumped conductors with performers.

Every group, every orchestra must have its leader. And leader and conductor are generally used interchangeably. However, "leader" actually connotes "boss," while "conductor" indicates the man who directs the performance. The leader may or may not play with the group; he may or may not conduct, but almost invariably he is in charge of the men, and he or one of his employees has the power to hire or fire them. The conductor, if he has the power to hire and fire, usually enjoys this power indirectly through someone else. He is a specialist whose primary functions are to mold and direct musical performances. In the fields of concert, opera, and ballet music, while the conductor may be a brilliant instrumentalist, he is rarely called upon to be both conductor and instrumentalist simultaneously. There are, of course, instances where this virtuoso stunt is executed—as, for example, when a man plays the solo part in a concerto and conducts the orchestra's performance at the same time. Needless to say, this is quite difficult, and the results are, on the whole, unsatisfactory.

Since leaders are, in a sense, entrepreneurs, it takes a certain amount of business initiative to become a leader. Conductors, on the other hand, are usually hired or appointed, and only rarely do the profits of the orchestra (if there are any) go directly to the conductor, but almost always the leader's profits are what remains after expenses. Job opportunities are limited by the number of orchestras that are functioning. The only exceptions are the few guest conductors and the accompanists who serve as guest conductors. Although conductors and leaders without orchestras cannot be said to be pursuing careers any more than painters without canvas or paints, there is nothing to prevent the hopeful young man from organizing his own orchestra, provided he has the initiative, the determination, the qualifications, the popular appeal (or a flair for it), and the wherewithal to start out and weather the early storms. (I will discuss all of this in more detail in a later chapter.)

Music writers' activities fall into three basic categories—composing, arranging, and copying. At times, one man may serve in two or more functions, but in most instances these functions are kept separate and are performed by different people.

Every tune that is played, whistled, or sung must first have been composed by someone, and every orchestra that is playing from music is utilizing the combined efforts of composer, arranger, and copyist. The field of composition is the most difficult of all in which to become established, but because of the principles of royalties and guaranteed performance rights, it can be quite lucrative, and the busy composer can provide himself with an ever-increasing income throughout his working life. There are several areas in which the composer can work, and the one he chooses will depend upon his talent, training, taste, and, above all, on the opportunities that are presented to him.

If he is (or proposes to be) primarily a songwriter, he will generally collaborate with a lyricist. Some songwriters write their own lyrics; others who write both words and music may collaborate with one or more people who write either or both. Some songs are the result of the joint efforts of several people. However, unless an unusual run of hits is envisioned, it is generally not profitable for more than three people to collaborate in songwriting. Most songs are written by two people—one a composer and the other a lyricist. The broadest markets for songwriters are found in the record industry, in motion pictures, and in musical shows of the Broadway musical comedy type.

Other commercial opportunities for composers exist in writing background music for movies and TV shows as well as for TV commercial spots. While it is not absolutely necessary for composers of background music to be skillful orchestrators, it is of inestimable advantage, and most successful film composers have not only a flair for the orchestra but are brilliant orchestrators.

One field that is generally not too well known is becoming increasingly profitable because of the tremendous growth of interest in music in public schools and colleges throughout the country. This is the field of educational music. Most large publishing houses now have educational music departments devoted to providing music of many different kinds for orchestras and bands that are organized and run by music departments in thousands of grade schools, high schools, and colleges. Much of this is original music written by composers who work directly for the publishers and are paid fee plus royalties. (Some are also paid a small weekly retainer.) Frequently, this music is written in several versions, varying only in degree of difficulty. In addition, composers thus associated with publishers, if they are expert orchestrators, write simplified versions of the standard repertoire for school use; and it is not unlikely for music published by other departments (popular, classical, or religious), music which shows promise of wide acceptance by schools, to be given an educational department version.

These assignments generally fall to the composers and arrangers who have been doing other work for the educational departments. Because of the rise in popularity of school choirs and glee clubs, educational departments of music publishing houses also provide a wide variety of choral music, and if the composers and arrangers commonly used are proficient in choral writing they get these assignments also, as well as assignments for combinations of orchestra and chorus. Often, however, choral assignments go to a specialist in choral work, and many well-known choral men and women write original compositions as well as arrangements of the standard literature for publication by educational departments. That the need for educational music has been expanding by leaps and bounds gives promise that many fine careers can be profitably pursued in this field.

The serious art composer has the most trying time of all. He must have unusual creative talent and an unswerving dedication to his art. Even with these attributes, his early career will almost certainly be hampered by the problems of getting his work performed and accepted. And, having persevered and won recognition as a master many years, and probably many symphonies, later, he will still be faced with the problem of earning an income for himself and his family. He will probably teach as a means of securing his livelihood, for no serious art composer, no matter how gifted or famous, is able, under present conditions and despite grants, gifts, and scholarship aid, to earn a respectable living in this country from his compositions alone. Composing is an excellent field for the individual who doesn't have full responsibility for supporting themselves or their families. It is therefore suitable for many married women and there have been some good, but largely unknown women composers.

For the person who needs to earn a living wage, however, composing appears to place one in an intolerable situation, for it really doesn't seem right for artists of such outstanding merit to have to seek other means to supplement their income. But many of them reap a harvest that, to them, has far greater value than any material reward. What can take the place of the admiration and respect they have earned from musical scholars, musicians, and music lovers? And is it not a life well spent to give vent to the simmering cauldron of creative drives that beset these men, to compose the music that may thrill countless generations?

It is unfortunate that for most of the masters their greatest adulation comes only after that last lingering spark of genius has been extinguished, after their deaths. But there is some satisfaction to be gained from the hope that their names and their music will live on after they are gone. And if any of these men is truly a master, a composer with a genius for invention and innovation, he can take much comfort from the knowledge that he has not only made a significant contribution to the musical literature and, therefore, to the culture of the world, but that he has helped to fashion the direction that music to come will take, and that his works will serve as models for the inspiration of the composers of the future.

When we speak of the world of arrangers and orchestrators, we speak of respected members of the musical society, who, in many instances, are capable of earning splendid livings. All music played by orchestras, bands, and combos is either arranged or orchestrated. Some arrangements are known as "head" arrangements, where the parts are conceived by the musicians themselves at rehearsals, never written down, but kept in their heads and played from memory in much the same manner every time. Other arrangements are said to be "faked." This is where the men, usually in small groups, are all familiar with the tune and the harmony being played; by listening carefully to each other and by signal and sign, they decide among themselves who will play the melody or a variation of it, one or more harmony parts that fit, or even an obbligato line. But all other music played by orchestras has been previously written out for them by either an arranger or an orchestrator.

In serious art music, as previously stated, the orchestration is most often written by the composer himself. However, in almost all forms of so-called commercial music this work is done by a man who undertakes either to orchestrate or arrange the music to be performed. A large body of this music is arranged or orchestrated for publishers and is printed in the form of "stock" arrangements. These are inexpensive ways for orchestras to acquire repertoire material and they are written in such a manner as to be adaptable to the needs of groups of different sizes.

Most of the rest of the orchestrations and arrangements that are written are known as "specials" and are written on specific orders for individual orchestras. Special arrangements make up the bulk, if not the entirety of the libraries of namedance bands and concert jazz orchestras of the Woody Herman type. Most of the arrangements used on commercial recordings are specials. The big variety and musical TV shows have staffs of arrangers to provide the music they require. Many singers, dancers, and entertainers have special arrangements written for their acts. In fact, almost everywhere that there is live music there is a need for the services of arrangers or orchestrators. But because of the serious inroads that taped music has made on live music, many expert arrangers and orchestrators are faced with little or no demand for their services. Some may be very busy for a few weeks and then find themselves unemployed for protracted periods. However, those lucky arrangers whose shows stay on the air year after year, or whose employers continue to have enough work to assign them are in a most enviable position and earn excellent incomes.

Copyists make up the remaining people in the music writing field. Although some composers orchestrate their own works, few of them do their own copying. And although some arrangers and orchestrators copy their own scores, copying is really a specialty by itself. The successful copyist must be fast, accurate, and extremely legible. His work consists of extracting the individual players' parts from the scores of the arrangers and orchestrators. The parts he writes are the actual parts from which the players perform the music. Busy copyists earn good money, but the amount of work available to them is dependent upon the amount of work available to their arrangers and orchestrators. A few copyists who have established copying services (businesses specializing in supplying copying service to anyone who needs it) have built up extensive and varied clienteles (TV shows, Broadway musical comedies, industrial shows, night club revues, operatic and symphony works, etc.) and have carved out splendid, well-paying careers for themselves.

In a field fraught with hazards, the area of teaching seems to offer the greatest security. For the teacher who gives private instruction, the opportunity for developing warmly personal teacher-student relationships can open the door to a thriving practice. However, the trend in the 1970's has been a faster increase in the number of public school teachers than in the number of pupils. Teachers are also better qualified than ever before. In the past decade the number of teachers holding bachelor's degrees has more than doubled and those holding master's and doctor's degrees has nearly tripled. All this contributes to making teaching a more competitive and less secure field than it used to be. Also, average salaries for music teachers (as for the whole teaching profession) are disappointingly low. Nevertheless, it is true that enough teachers who give private lessons, mainly in the principal cities, and who develop commanding reputations, have such busy schedules and charge such good fees that a career of this sort becomes a worthwhile and rewarding objective. Still, we must not forget that the vast majority of music teachers, regardless of where they teach, find it necessary to play or write to supplement their incomes. Some school systems do not pay too badly, and, combined with other efforts, help to provide a handsome income, but none pays well. It is not until we reach the top levels of university teaching at a mere handful of American colleges that teachers' salaries become realistic for this day and age.

The picture in schools devoted exclusively to the teaching of music varies with the individual school and with the reputation of the individual teacher as well as with the demand for his services. Another factor that enters into this picture is whether he is engaged as a full-time teacher with a full schedule of classes or as a private instructor for the school, and gives lessons on a more or less part-time basis.

Scholarships awarded to students at such privately endowed schools as Curtis, in Philadelphia, and Juilliard, in New York, defray, for the most part, the high fees charged by their teachers for private instruction. Schools with little or no scholarship funds to disperse can charge no more than the traffic will bear, for the onus of meeting instruction costs falls directly on the student, his family, or, possibly, his benefactors. Therefore, most teachers in these more typical schools are unable to command as high fees as those charged in the very top schools. But, there are no hard and fast rules. Men of outstanding reputation add prestige to any kind of school and usually set fees commensurate with their reputations.

There is another breed of music school that, because of its moderate rates and because most people want to learn to play an instrument, or at least because most parents want their children to learn to play an instrument, flourishes in this country. These schools sometimes specialize in one particular instrument, as, for instance, the accordion schools that have sprung up everywhere, or they may engage teachers to teach whatever instruments are in demand. Many of these schools perform a valuable service to their students, charge moderate rates, and maintain a good quality of instruction. Others charge very low rates, use inferior teachers, and engage in unethical practices, particularly with regard to the sale of instruments to their students. While the teachers in these schools may earn poor to fair incomes, the owners, who usually began as teachers themselves, are in a position to build large, blooming businesses. Chains of such schools, occasionally stretching across the country, pour a percentage of every lesson given into the owners' tills, and elevate this type of enterprise to the category of sizable business.

It can readily be seen that there are a large number of areas in which the musician may practice his craft. Some musicians choose their areas; others go where opportunity beckons. Musicians as a group are talented people, and many of them experience little difficulty in becoming proficient in several areas. Numerous musicians find their talents extending to other fields; many paint, write, or sculpt. Some find careers in fields totally unrelated to music. Others become involved in areas that have to do with music but are not within the spectrum of activities literally defined as musical.

Although most musicians specialize in one area of musical activity exclusively, a large number of musicians, either by choice or necessity, earn their livings by a combination of playing, writing, and teaching. The multifaceted nature of the musician's craft and the opportunity for developing and practicing versatility provide the musician with a lifetime full of challenges that are ever new and fresh. Moreover, it can free him from the boredom of performing the same activities day after day, from the deadly monotony that characterizes so many other fields.

CHAPTER II

Few Are Chosen

It is estimated that about three of every hundred music students go on to professionalism. This is an awesome figure when one considers the huge annual increases in the numbers of music students throughout the country. If this percentage were to remain constant, and if music education were to win national acceptance in school curriculums at the intensive level that prevails in England, it would be easy to foresee an army of four to five million professional musicians in America alone.

The chances are that each of those destined for professional careers has indulged, at some time or other, in some fanciful daydreams. The student has studied his instrument for a couple of years. He has made rapid strides by virtue of what appears to be a remarkable gift. He is awakening to the splendors of music. He has read glorious tales of music and musicians, past and present. His instructor has become justly proud of him and devotes extra time and attention to his progress. The student's appetite for reading, listening, and practicing is whetted by the instructor's recounting of personal experiences with world-famous artists, or of stories drawn from what he has read or heard. The student eagerly attends concerts and recitals. He gets caught up in the enthusiasm the audience displays for the performers. It seems that nothing in this world can ever be as thrilling as to perform beautiful and exciting music on the concert stage and to receive the plaudits of a grateful audience.

The fires have now been lit and the dreams begin in earnest. He is on the stage of Alice Tully Hall. Every seat is filled. Even the aisles are jammed with worshippers eager to hang on his every note. Everywhere he looks he is greeted by a sea of faces. The hush that precedes his first measures and continues to the end of each composition, mute testimony to the rapt attention of his audience, fills him with the rare exultation experienced only by performing artists. The tumultuous applause that greets the end of each piece and, finally, the shouts of "Bravo!" and "Encore!" from an audience, at last awakened from its hypnotic trance and unable to contain its ecstasy at his mastery, are more than adequate compensation for his work and dedication.

The rave notices are quickly followed by more triumphs at home and then abroad. Fortune follows fame, and repeat performances are followed by invitations to lecture and to write articles, books, and compositions. The world is his as honor after honor is heaped upon him. The numerous command performances before royalty attest to the magic of his name, while the world's reverence of him is an acknowledgement of his mastery of his art.

These are beautiful dreams, aren't they? To suggest that such dreams do not come true would be inaccurate. But to suggest that such fulfillment is the norm would be gross overstatement. There are, perhaps, three dozen men and women for whom such dreams have materialized in this century. All other artists are, alas, lumped together and relegated to lesser rank.

One name stands foremost among the artists of our time. One man will always be regarded as one of the greatest masters of the century. That man is Jascha Heifetz. Once, during a television interview, Heifetz was asked to state what he considered to be the most important qualities that make for success. His reply was "Self-respect, integrity, and enthusiasm." Keeping abreast of American tendencies toward oversimplification and the reduction of all ideas to irreducible minimums, he expressed, in those few words, what men have written and pondered for ages. And he hit the nail squarely on the head. Of course, such qualities as physical strength, fortitude and talent are implicit in his brief colloquy. But since such words do not give us a "how-to" approach, let us explore the process of becoming a concert artist.

The aspiring concert artist must have three loves. He must love his instrument; he must love music; and, above all, he must love people.

He must be judicious in his choice of a teacher, and should not shrink from inquiring after his teacher's qualifications and background. (There is good reason for doing this in the United States, where anyone, qualified or not, may, without restrictions of any kind, teach privately, whereas in Great Britain no one who has not been passed upon by a board of examiners may teach.) The student must be made to realize early that his teacher does not and cannot teach him anything in the sense of his being able to transfer knowledge from his own mind directly into that of the student's. Instead, the teacher stimulates the student's mind to wish to learn and suggestively presents to the student that material which is both desirable and necessary to be learned.

Only after the student demonstrates his receptivity and willingness to learn can the teacher help him to learn. Then, firmly but gently, he guides the student, encourages him to develop and use his imagination and to express his own individuality. In the final analysis, it is the student himself who, by his own efforts, does the learning. The teacher shows him how to analyze the things he plays, how to treat the details while keeping the broad shape and outline of the composition as a whole in mind, and gives him sound musical reasons in support of the logicality of one conception as opposed to the illogicality of another. Further, his instructor helps him to develop good physical and mental habits before bad habits can creep in, and endeavors to expose and caution him to avoid those incorrect practices that otherwise will tend to become fixed as bad habits.

The teacher plays for the student in conjunction with explanation rather than solely for the purpose of providing an example for imitation, and he exercises those niceties of judgment that are the very things the student needs most to learn, for if these were his in the first place he would scarcely require a teacher at all. The teacher helps him to perceive what it is that renders a musical performance

good, or the reverse, to perceive what is essential and what is un-
essential both in his own playing and in that of others. Above all,
he insists that his student listen attentively to himself at all times and
never practice or play a piece through without the express purpose
of knowing it better—knowing it better musically, knowing it better
technically.

Having found a teacher who can give him all this and more, the
potential artist should encounter no insurmountable obstacle to the
mastery of the technical difficulties of his instrument. But he must
remember that practicing is work, hard work, and progress is never
made by leaps and bounds even by the most gifted. His love for his
instrument must be so great that regardless of the sacrifices involved,
regardless of the time and energy expended, it will lead him un-
erringly to his first goal, mastery of his instrument.

Ruskin once said, "Nothing that is great is easy." Unfortunately,
the desire to become an artist accomplishes nothing unless it provides
the impetus for doing something about it. It is only the determination and the patience to work unremittingly toward the goal that
proves the sincerity of the desire, the nature of the love. These, and
these alone, bring the looked-for results.

This writer does not propose to tell the prospective virtuoso how
much he should practice each day. That is strictly a matter for him
to decide. However, music students whose ambition it is to become
professionals are urged to practice three or four hours daily, and
those planning on a concert career generally need to be coaxed from
their practicing after daily sessions of six to ten hours, although they
are frequently permitted to increase these practice periods on weekends.

Regarding the many years of drudgery required to begin to approach artistic perfection, the following quotations seem especially
appropriate. The first is credited to several people and points directly
to the one factor that scholars through the ages have thought to be
responsible for bringing to flower the work of gifted and promising
individuals. "Genius is nothing but a great aptitude for taking pains."
Then, there is its paraphrase in verse:

"Genius, that power which dazzles mortal eyes
Is oft but perseverance in disguise."

We do not accept the view that "a great aptitude for taking pains" is actually a definition of genius, but we feel the urgency of driving home this one point: genius must necessarily be accompanied by an infinite capacity for patience and taking pains or the divine gift will only wilt on the vine and never bloom to perfection.

The second love required of the artist is the love for music. This, too, covers a lot of ground. The artist must master a large segment of the literature of his instrument. This means not just committing to memory a sizable repertoire, but rather, as part of the process of learning and memorizing, constantly analyzing the compositions being studied. He must know every detail of every piece he studies. He must know its form and structure. He must know every phrase, every theme, motive, or fragment, and in what manner ensuing uses of this material differ, if at all, from that of its original statement. He must be aware of every contrapuntal, rhythmic, or harmonic device employed by the composer. He must recognize every shift of tonality, no matter how fleeting, and come to understand the composer's reasons for these modulations. He should know which passages constitute bridge material and how each fits into the total scheme of the composition. He should understand the principles of variety and contrast of thematic material, and he should learn to communicate these contrasts in his own playing without distorting any of the musical quality for the sake of emphasis. He should know which material is derivative and he should recognize the source of all such derivative material used in developments and codas despite the ingenuity of composers for concealing the fact that such material is derivative, and, at the same time, he must be able to distinguish between old and new material.

And, by the manner of his playing, he must be able to convey all of this information to his listeners. In addition, he should show a great awareness of the use of new harmonies and new orchestral devices (those which differ from the harmonies and orchestration of the original statements of the themes) in the restatement of thematic material. And he must demonstrate an exquisite sensitivity to tonal and architectural balance.

The aspiring concert artist must know all these things plus the dozens of other tools of the composer's craft, and learn to recognize each in the compositions he studies and hears. In short, he must become a master at the analysis of composition, although he need not himself be a composer.

This knowledge is revealed to the student only through the intensive study of each composition, never through a mere mechanical memorization of a work. The ability to analyze so meticulously presupposes a thorough knowledge of harmony, counterpoint, orchestration, fugue, musical form, and even the history of music. This last is the special prerequisite for the performing artist, but is it not through the knowledge of what preceded, followed, and was contemporary with a particular work that we gain an insight into what is new, daring, and imaginative in this composition, what is traditional, and what, stylistically speaking, would or would not be acceptable in its performance?

The history of music teaches us the limitations imposed on the composer by such things as the state of development of the orchestra and orchestration technique, the state of development of the commonly used instruments, the state of instrumental virtuosity, as well as the commonly accepted harmonic and contrapuntal practices of the period. Even the knowledge of the life and times of the individual composer is essential to our understanding of his music. And it is not too much to say that the intimate details of a composer's life, which surrounded the creation of his compositions, his state of maturity, his state of mind and of health provide clues to the performance of his works and, in many instances, supply the only available keys to their faithful interpretation.

The budding concert artist will have begun at an early age to learn representative compositions of the great masters and will continue, as rapidly as possible, to extend the breadth and depth of his knowledge of the literature. By the time he is ready for the concert stage, he should be acquainted with most of the literature written for his instrument, and he should have mastered much of it. Besides, he should have a wide knowledge of all musical literature, whether written for his instrument or not. And this knowledge should be increased and broadened throughout his life.

A few words of warning seem appropriate at this juncture. The concert artist of today is a product of today and, as such, must be attuned to his own times. In fact, it is the intellectuals and artists of the day who, in large measure, by their explorations of the unknown and the untried, set the tone of the times, and the concert artist must be identified as belonging to his own times; he must stimulate and be stimulated by the leaders of his day. He must not be forever looking backward. It is one thing to know and revere the works of the past, to appreciate in full measure the great masters who preceded us, but it is quite another thing to judge the music of today by the standards applied to the music of yesterday and to allow our love for the latter to circumscribe our sympathy for the former.

It is amazing that so many excellent teachers who are thrilled by what shocked the audiences of Beethoven, Brahms, or Wagner, are disturbed by the practices of contemporary composers. Many of them, in their youth, applauded the radical practices of young composers, but, as they grew older, they became more conservative and shut the gates of their minds to new ideas. Contributing to this mental cloture may be the fact that it is much easier for them to teach compositions with which they have had years of familiarity than to try to evaluate and explain contemporary music. They are on much safer ground in analyzing and interpreting those compositions that have stood the test of time and proved their greatness than in attempting to fathom the complexity and the dissonant quality of a large body of modern music, music which departs in substance and in texture from older models, music which they prefer to believe does not exist at all.

Of course, this does not apply to all good teachers, for many habitually learn and teach new compositions. But too many succumb to conservatism as they grow older; steeped in the past, they become victims of traditionalism. This settling down, this search for roots in the past, this opposition to change may be explained away as a normal accompaniment to growing older. However, since new ideas generate an atmosphere conducive to mental activity of a high order, their exclusion can only lead to stifling our intellectual growth, and regardless of the natural tendency toward conservatism as we grow older, it is a course to be vigorously resisted.

Many teachers, therefore, attempt, wittingly or not, to inculcate their students with a love for the past and its products while cultivating their disdain for new works. The student must not fall into the trap of being thus influenced, and the concert artist, to be worthy of the name, must outgrow the intellectual limitations of his teacher, whenever and wherever these manifest themselves. He must know that the music of today has validity for today and that many contemporary composers are producing works of high artistic merit, works that in a later age will come to be known as representative of our time. He must comprehend and love this music, too, and eagerly accept the role not only of being the interpreter of the works of the past, but of being one who communicates the artistic expression of the writers of today to the audiences of today. He must champion today's music. Otherwise, it may lie unperformed and undiscovered until a later day or, worse yet, for all eternity.

I hear voices querulously demanding, "What about Chopin specialists, Beethoven specialists, Mozart specialists? What about men whose lives are devoted to the study and interpretation of the music of Bach? What about lovers of musica antiqua?" So I must digress to answer these complainers.

These men provide something very special for music. They give us authoritative and scholarly interpretations of the works of those masters to whom they have devoted their artistic lives. Several of these men can trace their student-teacher lineage directly back to the composers of their choice. Their position in music is as much that of the musical scholar as the performing artist. The models they supply establish and keep alive standards of performance and interpretation, which comprise a storehouse of reliable information that the whole world may draw from. Thus, they contribute much to musical scholarship and pass this knowledge on to their students.

It is conceded that Bach's sedulousness resulted in such a mammoth outpouring of music that it is a challenge to any man, given a normal life span, to become a Bach specialist. Yet, no specialist ever concertizes from the works of one composer exclusively, or even from the works of one era exclusively. Of course, if one plays an ancient instrument for which nothing has been written for a hundred and fifty years, he would be hard pressed to play a modern work. But this writer feels that the master of the modern instrument who plays the works of the dear dead past exclusively, however well he may bring them to life, is so woefully dated he cannot be identified with current musical philosophy. Further, he contends that the modern artist has an obligation to bring today's music to the audiences of today. As Samuel Taylor Coleridge once said, "No models of the past times, however perfect, can have the same vivid effect on the mind as the productions of contemporary genius." By fulfilling this obligation, the artist serves two excellent purposes: He acquaints his audiences with the fruits of contemporary musical thinking, and he provides young composers with the opportunity to be heard.

The aspiring young artist should expose himself to musical performance at every opportunity. He should habitually attend concerts, recitals, operas, and all other kinds of musical events. Recitals serve a particularly important function to the young artist, since they give him a firsthand knowledge of good programming and pacing. He must learn why certain combinations of compositions constitute effective programs and where in the program each composition should be placed. By observing the programs of other artists, he should grasp the significance of the principles of variety and contrast that are so important in the selection of compositions to be played.

Attendance at recitals gives the aspirant the opportunity to take part in the musical experience that is destined to become such a large part of his life. There is no substitute for the live performance, neither from the standpoint of emotional impact nor from the standpoint of a careful study of every aspect of the performance. Clearly, the young man planning a concert career can ill afford to neglect any avenue of study that is open to him. There is no detail of performance whose improvement will not aid the individual's chances for success, and regular attendance at recitals will furnish the perceptive listener with an impressive list of dos and don'ts to add to his daily schedule of things to think about and practice.

There is a great wealth of material on phonograph records and tapes, and the aspiring young artist should avail himself of the opportunity to study closely those performances worthy of study. Unfortunately, as much of this is mediocre as it is excellent, and it requires a highly discriminating mind to determine which performances are of high artistic calibre. In this case, reliance on one's teacher's judgment should prove of inestimable advantage.

Nowadays, the most sophisticated equipment can, in effect, put the listener right in the middle of the New York Philharmonic. Fifteen years ago stereo appeared on the scene and now, with the availability of four-channel (quadraphonic) sound, recordings can have depth as well as length and breadth. The four separate channels can be recreated both on tapes and on disks. However, though stereo tapes and disks and the equipment on which to play them are within the budgets of many, quadrophonic sound is still in the future for most of us. Except for those with the very latest equipment, only a carefully executed live performance allows one to hear and follow every detail of the score. Nevertheless, records and tapes serve as an excellent auxiliary to music study; they permit an intimate knowledge of compositions and their interpretations to be gained through repeated playings, and make possible the most minute observation of details by repetition of individual passages.

The third love that must consume the concert artist is his love for people. Robert Schumann once asked, "What is the musician's calling? Is it not to send light into the deep recesses of the human heart?" And we ask, What is the artist's calling if not to be middleman between the composer and the listener? Is it not for him to recreate the products of the composer's imagination and to bring the joy of music to the ears and hearts of his fellows? The ability to communicate with clarity and warmth is dependent not only upon his perception of the material he wishes to deliver but upon his love and respect for his audience, which, however cloaked, manifest themselves as a tremendous enthusiasm for performing. The performer's three loves, especially his love for people, are in evidence the moment he enters the stage. Like some form of telepathy, his love communicates itself instantly and heightens the listeners' receptivity to the message about to be conveyed, or, should this love be lacking or fail to be adequately transmitted, the audience senses this deficiency immediately and becomes hostile, unreceptive, and difficult to please.

We submit that there have been those artists who have flaunted their skill and musical superiority and have scorned the intelligence of their audiences. We further submit that there have been artists whose reputations as eccentrics have surrounded them with auras of glamour, and we grant that such men have achieved notable success. But can the reader deny that such seemingly tasteless behavior mannerisms may be only gambits and ploys, well calculated to command attention and designed to make easier the rapport that the artist has to achieve if he is to communicate at all? We doubt that any sincere artist concertizes merely to parade his virtuosity or that ego gratification and exhibitionism are his sole motivating forces. We believe that any sincere artist has within him the desire to bring his treasures to appreciative and attentive audiences, to cast a light into the recesses of their hearts. What is it, then, if not love that impels the artist to share his musical riches with them?

These three loves, of themselves, are not enough to bring the artist continuing triumph. Two more ingredients are indispensable to his success at the box office. They are elusive, intangible, and difficult to explain, yet they are absolutely essential to the artist if he is to maintain his popularity year after year.

In his massive tract, "The Arts," Hendrik Willem Van Loon wrote the following: "There exists an innermost belief among musical beginners that if they are only good enough and work hard and faithfully, they will eventually be able to draw large crowds and break the records of Jenny Lind or Paderewski. I hate to upset the faith of the younger generation in the inevitable triumph of good intentions. Far be it from me to let them suspect, even for a moment, that anything can be accomplished in this world without a tremendous amount of hard work and a great deal of natural talent. But the history of the concert stage of the last hundred years seems to indicate that those qualities alone are not enough. One other element is just as necessary. It is not luck, though a little bit of good luck should never be despised. But what is needed for an overwhelming success is a combination of legitimate showmanship with a dash of what the Germans used to call *Bühnentalent*. It is not easy to give the exact translation of that word. 'Talent for the stage' is a little too weak. It really means ability to put it over, that mysterious something that establishes an immediate contact between the public in the house and the artist at the other side of the footlights. This *Bühnentalent* is something different in the case of every performer."

Van Loon went on to tell us that Paderewski, a natural-born showman, had a magical appeal to his public. The same was true of Fritz Kreisler, who was anything but a showman. In fact, Kreisler was, he noted, the "personification of unassuming simplicity." On the other hand, Jan Kubelik, who was a brilliant artist, was unable to "maintain his hold upon the public."

Van Loon believed that a few clever stage managers and musical agents knew the secret, and that Hollywood, too, knew and used the secret over and over again. The answer—cleverly surrounding their stars with a nimbus of glamour.

"Glamour," according to the dictionary, means "a magical or fictitious beauty attached to any person or object—a delusion or alluring charm." Actual physical beauty has nothing to do with it. Tremendous intellectual ability is not in the least necessary. Absolute mastery of the instrument is, of course, a *sine qua non*. Hard work and an infinite willingness to take infinite pains are also indispensable. But over and beyond this there must be the gift of magic—the ability to make people feel that there is more there than they can see or hear, something that keeps them curious and interested and makes them look for an answer without ever being able to find it."

Actually, Van Loon was writing about two separate things, *Bühnentalent* and glamour, and he lumped them together under the term of glamour. But glamour is undeniably one of the important ingredients of success.

It is not within the scope of this book to discuss fully the term "glamour" or to instruct the young artist in how to become glamorous. An imaginative press agent and a clever manager can probably do more for him than any writer, especially since each artist's case is different and so must be handled individually.

The ability to put it across, to exert a hypnotic effect upon audiences—in short, to have them eating out of your hand, that other necessary element, however nebulous a talent it may appear to be—is of such importance to the solo performer, the conductor, and others in the public eye that a few words on the subject are deemed worth writing. I know a brilliant violist whose artistry ranks with the world's best, but, despite his acknowledged artistry, his lack of personal magnetism causes him to fail as a popular favorite wherever he goes. This one failing and this only will always prevent his becoming a top-drawing performer.

Some performers are gifted with stagemanship. (I prefer to use that word to describe *Bühnentalent* and personal magnetism. "Showmanship" suggests something a trifle more flamboyant and vulgar than I intend.) Give them a few years of experience and they know exactly what to do to fire a crowd with enthusiasm. In years gone by, when vaudeville and burlesque houses flourished all over the country, entertainers had a marvelous training ground for developing this talent. Even those without natural gifts for the stage learned by doing and observing, and there remained, when vaudeville disappeared, a large group of performers who possessed an unquestioned mastery of stagemanship. Since the end of vaudeville, the opportunities for learning by doing have dwindled remarkably. Consequently, the high levels of stagemanship achieved by many stars of a bygone era are nowadays only rarely equaled.

The concert artist, on the other hand, had no such intensive training ground as the two-a-day. In matters of stagemanship, he was largely left to his own devices, and in most cases it was considered beneath the dignity of an artist to seek out artificial aids to casting a spell upon audiences. And, anyway, it was considered a God-given gift. If you had it, all well and good, but if you did not, there was nothing to be done about it, no way to acquire it. Nonsense! The most intelligent artists have always recognized its value and have sought in one way or another to develop the desired qualities. Franz Liszt learned and remembered much from watching Paganini. He did not stoop to the charlatanism of which Paganini was guilty, but instead he so skillfully applied to his own personality and deportment the knowledge gained from his observations that he became the most glamorous, most magnetic, and most sought-after musical figure of his time.

Some men emit an irresistible magnetism the moment they stride into a room full of people. Some artists grip their audiences in similar manner the instant they stride upon the stage. A quick smile from such men and their audiences swoon. These men are never thought to walk into a room or to step upon a stage. They stride. We are prone to dramatize their every motion.

I shall not state categorically that each of us can develop a personal magnetism commensurate with that of the world's most charming people. But all successful artists have traits of personality and behavior that instantly strike responsive chords in their listeners. Hindemith has written to the effect that there are no patterns of human thought or behavior that through intelligent and diligent investigation cannot be divined. And after reading Vance Packard's provocative *The Hidden Persuaders,* I felt more confidently than ever before that the image of himself that a man projects can be molded into a shape that will come at least close to producing the desired effect.

What does all this mean to the young concert artist? We must assume that he is both highly intelligent and sensitive to many things so subtle or esoteric that they are hardly perceived by less gifted people. By using these gifts wisely, he can accomplish much in the direction of bearing, manner, personality, deportment, magnetism—in short, toward stagemanship.

As noted earlier, the young artist is encouraged to attend as many concerts and recitals as possible. With the object of acquiring a knowledge of stagemanship, he should consciously refrain from becoming immersed in the music, but should carefully observe every mannerism, gesture, facial expression, and so forth of the artist who is performing. He should pay particular attention to the artist-audience relationship at various points during the concert. He should attempt to discern what in particular affected this relationship, which visible manifestations were effective and which were ineffective, and, if possible, which invisible components of his stagemanship contributed to this relationship. He should form a mental graph of this interaction and attempt to deduce some principles from his observations.

He should apply this procedure to dozens of artists who perform in as many different media as possible (concert hall, small auditorium, private music room, opera house, movies, and TV), and he should see each artist as often as possible in order to note consistency or variations in stage deportment. He might even be able to determine if variations in behavior were caused by audience stimuli. He should check all of his findings with each other to see if some common principles can be evolved.

He should play for people as often as possible—informal get-togethers, parties, school events, local concerts, any place at all where he may have an audience. As soon as he has acquired enough confidence in his playing, he should begin to play with one ear on his music and the other on his audience. In other words, he should begin to be conscious of his effect on them and theirs on him, and he should begin to use some of the knowledge he has gained from observing other artists. He should experiment with one thing and another, always judging its effect on people. He should discard ineffective or antagonistic devices and develop the effective principles of stagemanship into firm habits. As his knowledge, experience, and mastery increase, he will have made much progress toward the goal of being able to cast a hypnotic spell upon his audiences, and he will have learned much about that mystifying entity, personal popularity.

We grant that personal appeal and popularity have much more to do with a man's popularity than with his artistic worth, but it is that popularity, more than anything else, that keeps the cash customers clamoring for tickets at the box office. And I never heard of an unpopular artist who gained either affluence or influence.

Two men of widely different fields, with differing approaches, both paragons of stagemanship, come to mind as being particularly worthy of observation. These men are Leonard Bernstein and Frank Sinatra. Each enjoys unquestioned popularity (in 1973 audiences paid a record $30 to hear Sinatra at a Las Vegas dinner show—his first major appearance after a two year absence); each has the ability to captivate his audience. Leonard Bernstein begins with a simple direct appeal to the emotions and intellects of his audience. Then, by gradually increasing the dramatic impact, by a sustained emotional crescendo, he sweeps his listeners (and watchers) on to rapturous heights. His pacing, whether he is delivering a lecture, conducting a concert, or playing the piano is so well calculated that he never fails to overwhelm his audiences.

Sinatra, on the other hand, is a man of rapidly changing moods. He is first arrogant, then tender, lowly, funny, forlorn, happy, then all of these things in quick succession. No sooner does his audience perceive one mood than it is forced to abandon it to identify with a different one. No mood is sustained for more than a couple of minutes. Sinatra, a master of stagemanship, transports his audience into a kaleidoscope of shifting emotional colors, and they love every minute of it.

The differences in the approach to stagemanship between Bernstein and Sinatra are caused not only by their differences in personality but by the nature of the material each wishes to convey. Nevertheless, each gets across what he has to say with such unmistakable clarity and warmth that his public finds him irresistible.

(The above does not purport to be a detailed analysis of the stagemanship of Leonard Bernstein or Frank Sinatra. It merely describes briefly and superficially a rudimentary and obvious difference in their techniques. Our purpose is to call attention to the importance of stagemanship as part of an artist's equipment and the necessity for giving more than a little thought to the means of achieving it. A thorough analysis of the techniques of stagemanship as employed by our foremost artists is left to the student until such time as some psychologically oriented author publishes an exhaustive study of the subject.)

If the young man planning on a concert career is fired by the love for his instrument and for music and by his love for people, revealed through his insatiable desire to play for them and through his constant efforts to evoke a warm and enthusiastic response from audiences, where shall he go to consummate these loves? Where shall he study after his preliminary musical education is complete? Is study abroad necessary, worthwhile, or desirable? What physical and mental qualities must he possess to be well disposed to a successful concert career? How does he go about making his debut and where?

Music education in America, particularly at the higher levels, is equal to, or surpasses, that of any other country in the world, and it is improving continually. We have more and better teachers and music schools than we have ever before had, and these, in turn, are turning out more graduates who are better trained to improve the standards of music education than this country has ever produced. There are so many excellent music schools and conservatories in America that to attempt to name them would be a disservice to those who might inadvertently be left out. There is scarcely a large city in the country that cannot boast of at least one excellent music school and a distinguished faculty. Many colleges and universities have splendid music departments, and those that offer courses in applied music are generally well equipped to prepare gifted instrumentalists for concert careers. Many of these fine schools offer full scholarships to applicants who qualify, while others admit only those to whom scholarships have been granted.

Students who wish to work toward a degree must be high school graduates and take competitive examinations to gain entrance to the better music schools. Colleges and universities also require matriculants to be high school graduates, but the other requirements to be met vary. Some require the C.E.E.B. (College Entrance Examination Board) examination plus a certain class standing or average. Others dispense with entrance examinations or give their own. Some colleges after granting admission require the student to demonstrate his proficiency by a series of auditions before permitting him to make music his major. Lovejoy's *College Guide* lists the address and a summary of entrance requirements of every accredited college and university in the country, and all of them send catalogues upon request. The music section of newspapers such as the Sunday *New York Times* will usually contain advertisements for a number of fine music schools.

Nowadays, practically every fine music school in the country produces its share of virtuosi, and the prospective concert artist is strongly advised to continue his musical education enrolled at the college level in a fine music school or in a liberal-arts college that has a superior music department.

It is not necessary to go abroad to study, but since a number of scholarships offer an opportunity to study abroad, both at the undergraduate and graduate level, it would be pointless for a recipient of one of these to turn it down. There is always something exciting about studying in a foreign country, something that stimulates one's intellectual curiosity, something that compels one to do one's best to prove to those at home that neither time nor money was wasted and that confidence was justified. Second, it is good for one to be exposed to fresh or different points of view, and it would be all but impossible in a foreign land not to come into contact with modes of thinking that differed from those to which one has grown accustomed. This would tend to broaden relatively parochial ideas and, at the same time, would provide an impetus for exploration of new paths. Third, studying abroad is of value because many, many people in this country are tremendously impressed by musicians who have studied abroad. Last, study abroad may provide the opportunity to begin a successful concert career abroad, and this, more than anything else, can open the door to a triumphant return to the United States. Yes, by all means study abroad if you get the chance. The word "abroad" still has a magical charm for millions of music lovers here at home.

By the time he is seventeen or eighteen, the prospective concert artist will usually have demonstrated such markedly superior talent that his gaining admission to a fine music school and his prospects for winning a scholarship competition will offer almost no problem at all. I say "almost" because it does not always follow that the most gifted win the prizes. No method requiring subjective judgment can ever be foolproof, and educators and test-makers are the first people to admit this. Also, it is just possible that our gifted lad (or lass) has been up against someone just as gifted as he, or perhaps he did not feel well or perform up to his level the day of the competition. But let us assume that, scholarship or not, he has joined the ranks of the students at the school of his choice. What qualities will his teachers look for in him if they believe him to be artist material? What qualities should he look for in himself?

Heifetz used the term "integrity." This is a must. It implies an honesty and objectivity in self-appraisal that prevents the student from ever being really satisfied with the quality of his work or his rate of progress. His honesty must demand that he compare his own playing with that of his colleagues, coolly and with as much detachment as is humanly possible. His integrity must never permit even a hint of narcissism in his self-analysis. He must possess both integrity and unusual talent; he must be introspective and industrious to a high degree.

Tobias Matthay wrote in *Musical Interpretation,* that "the really great artist always has been, is now, and ever will be a most rare phenomenon. His advent depends on so many things uniting in one single individual—the highest gifts of imagination and invention, therefore high mental powers (yes, the really great artist must also have high reasoning power), physical and mental endurance, extreme enthusiasm for his chosen art, good health, and the opportunities to acquire the requisite skill to work in strict obedience to the laws of his art."

There are literally hundreds completing their formal musical studies each year who appear to possess these qualifications. But what happens to them from this point on in their careers?

That handful of artists destined, because of extraordinary gifts, for greatness is able to perform in such breathtaking manner that, even lacking the extra-musical qualities outlined earlier in this chapter, audiences are overwhelmed and their infectious enthusiasm spreads in short order to all corners of the globe. A few years of exposure to an excited and eager public and this tiny group is elevated to a niche that befits such outstanding talent. Long, rewarding careers become a reality for them; wealth and prominence are realized as huge fees are demanded and received at every turn.

But what of the hundreds upon hundreds of other truly splendid artists who are richly endowed with talent and superb in their skills but who fall just short of greatness? For them the battle is really on and every resource at their command must be utilized to survive in this highly competitive area.

Certainly, there are scholarships to further their studies and prizes that give exposure in the form of recitals and guest appearances with reputable orchestras. Yet, these are not the final solutions to the problem of gaining a foothold in the concert world.

Not too many years ago, unless a concert artist was foreign born, he had very little chance of pursuing a successful career in this country. Things have changed and today he has some chance, but it is not particularly bright unless something noteworthy brings him to the attention of the concert-going public. The career of pianist Van Cliburn offers an excellent example. There was a time when he could not be sold on a Community Concerts program for a fee of a hundred and fifty dollars. But let some noted music critic, such as Nikita Khrushchev, hail his talents, and he is greeted as a celebrity in this country, toasted as a world-famed virtuoso, and priced right out of the small-time concert circuit.

One young violin virtuoso was called some years ago to play a recording date. It turned out to be a gimmick recording of the first movement of the Mendelssohn violin concerto, the gimmick being that eighteen top violinists in the free-lance field in New York, all artists in their own right, were to play the solo part in unison. Our young violinist, who had drifted into the free-lance field because the pickings in the concert field were meager and who, as the result of winning a highly prized violin competition, had played the Mendelssohn concerto all over Europe with the best orchestras as a reward for winning the competition, wryly noted that he had played the composition thirty times as a soloist in Europe and yet this was the first time he was to be paid for it.

The young artist needs exposure and exposure costs money. To give a recital, a hall must be rented. (In New York, Town Hall and Alice Tully Hall are fully booked, often by young hopefuls trying to impress the public and the press.) A recital at Alice Tully costs approximately $1400. Tickets and programs must be printed. Recitals must be publicized. Even the initial cost of a wardrobe and its maintenance is not to be considered trifling. If one's family cannot afford to provide substantial assistance, a sponsor or patron must be found who is interested in furthering the career of the young artist.

Many young artists work at other kinds of things to save the money necessary for a debut or for follow-up recitals. Some play in theatres or teach, or if they are lucky, they play the best free-lance work that is available. Others teach and, if they are married, husbands and wives pool their earnings to save enough money to give the recitals.

Many young artists mistakenly believe that if they receive some recognition in the form of winning competitions, some artist service will take them under its wings and help further their careers. But let's face it, booking agents, personal managers, and artists' services are not cultural institutions; they are motivated by profit, and, unless they see bright prospects of their 20 percent cut amounting to something sizable, they will not be interested in investing in the future of an unknown artist. (One artist, to my knowledge, was offered a South American concert tour provided he would pay six thousand dollars to the artist service to "help defray potential losses.")

Even those who find themselves able to afford to give recitals encounter difficulties that are often insurmountable. We are a nation supposedly famous for championing the underdog, and yet we have grown so accustomed to having fashion dictate our likes and dislikes and so spoiled by having our idols at our fingertips on records, television, and in the movies that we are prone to ignore the merits of the unknown artist. Indeed, we not only are too lazy to make the effort to appraise his work but, what is more tragic, we are largely incapable of making rational, significant evaluations.

In addition to this apathy on the part of the general public, the fledgling concert artist encounters a generally indifferent and hostile press. Music reviewers have a field day with debut concerts and, almost to a man, term the beginning artist's first recitals as "unpolished, rough, uneven, inept," and they use other choice adjectives that can only serve the purpose of scaring away cash customers and shaking the confidence of the unseasoned artist. First recitals are a signal for these writers to flex their rhetorical muscles with their tools of sarcasm, irony, wit, mockery, and even derision. Too many journalists, free to write as they please about musical events, know a good deal more about the English language than they could hope to know about music, yet they are given license to sow the seeds of failure and frustration for so many promising young artists. (Luckily for New York, the critics of its leading newspaper, *The New York Times,* are knowledgeable in musical matters and usually exercise enough restraint to be above reproach.)

Although we are a nation that traditionally spends more money on musical offerings than on baseball, many excellent artists are fated to have unsuccessful concert careers. Even if these unfortunates have been touched by the divine fire, living in cold garrets and subsisting on cold spaghetti will be of little consequence. As a result, those who are sensitive to the practical necessities of life frequently forego a concert career for something more immediate and substantial. They get into free-lance work, symphony orchestras, theatre orchestras, music education, or even out of the music field entirely. But no matter in which direction their careers take them, the world is the poorer for losing their services as concert artists.

The majority of concert artists who are considered fairly successful earn but modest incomes from concertizing. The more outstanding artists, of course, command larger fees and have larger followings. Those artists whose popularity places them in the class of "personalities" rank with the tiny handful of giants of the field who earn huge sums of money.

It is safe to say that the number of artists in the world who earn in excess of $50,000 a year would not fill all the top executive chairs of any large New York City office building, and yet if the people of whom the concert field consists could have devoted their talents and industry to almost any other field of endeavor, they would surely have reaped untold riches, far greater than they could ever have hoped for in music.

So much is expected of our concert artists that the advent of a truly great artist is surely a phenomenon, and yet no concert artists have ever earned as much money as any of that group of pop idols who were teen-age successes in the 1960's. To bring into proper perspective those few at the top of the pyramid whose incomes are very large, one must notice that the sides of the pyramid rest on a broad base of highly competent artists whose earning power is consistently lower than that of semi-skilled labor. And the increasing numbers of newcomers each year, better and better trained, wonderfully equipped to bring beautiful music to the ears of millions, form a never-ending source for replenishing and enlarging that base, a reservoir of human talent from which only an occasional one will be picked, sometimes almost like the winner of a lottery, to scale the walls and make the ascent to the apex.

CHAPTER III

The Symphony Musician

We Americans are justly proud of our great orchestras. We point to them as living proof of the vitality of culture in a free Western society. Most of us are not aware that our best orchestras are the finest in the world, that our land can boast of having a number of the most talented composers in the world, and that our outstanding young conductors will one day be among the world's most renowned. By and large, Americans do not really know this, but if the question were put to them, they would brashly declare it to be true. That is the kind of people Americans are—blindly confident of the talent of Americans.

Unfortunately, the majority of devoted concert-goers is as captivated by imported art and artists as it is by imported perfume and champagne. (Although today but a few American artists are regarded as highly as Europeans, the prejudice is being ever so slowly worn away.) The concert-going public could take a lesson from its brother Americans. This is a nation rich in human resources, and since so much of the cream of Europe's talent has taken up residence in this country, our native talent has profited immensely from exposure to wonderful models and superb instruction.

Who can fail to be impressed by the sight of a hundred men sitting on the stage, instruments poised, awaiting the point of the first downbeat? Who can fail to be impressed by the sound of a hundred men beginning as one and continuing on with perfect precision, guided by the seemingly undecipherable patterns set up by the baton?

Who can fail to be impressed by the sight of an army of bows marching up and down and across the strings like a crack drill team? Can
even the stranger to music fail to be carried away as the sonorities
soar and fill the hall, or change to a shimmer, now dancing back and
forth, now sparkling like a thousand gems, now rising once again
to a majestic crescendo?

Those men on the platform have devoted their lives to recreating
the monumental masterworks of the greatest musical minds that ever
existed. They have undergone the same rigorous discipline, the same
attention to detail that was part of the concert artist's training. Theirs
is a lofty cause—to give human expression to the cold, meaningless,
little notes they see before them, so that once again the emotion, the
vitality, the heavenly beauty that took shape in the master's mind
can bridge the void to become a fleeting reality and be sung out, as
by a thousand choruses, in all its glory.

Somewhere in that audience are two or three dozen talented young
men and women. They are students at the local conservatory. They
study diligently and their progress has been excellent. They will soon
be ready for important things. Their teachers are all players in the
symphony orchestra there on the stage. The students' ambitions have
remained unchanged for years. They wish to take their instruments,
leave the audience, and cross over to the stage, to sit in and join the
orchestra and take part in what for them is the greatest of all human
experiences.

What chances really have they of fulfilling their ambitions? In the
United States and Canada there are thousands of orchestras, quartets,
and chamber ensembles—amateur, semiprofessional, and professional. The students of the members of these groups at least have an
inside track in their aspirations. The recommendations of such
teachers can be weighty. So are the recommendations of non-
symphony teachers of high repute. Only the recommendations of
someone higher up on the totem pole carry greater weight.

If the ambition of our young men and women was to be engaged
by the symphony orchestra in which their teachers play, although
their chances are brighter than for most others, there would be little
reason for optimism that the big break will come soon. In fact, it

would be unrealistic to aim at any one particular orchestra unless encouragement was given as a result of an impending vacancy. The wisest procedure, if symphony orchestra it had to be, would be to take whatever position was forthcoming, regardless of where it was. The experience, even of playing with an inferior orchestra, would be valuable, and it would probably be worthwhile to keep such a position until such time that a job is offered in the home-town symphony. If the inferior orchestra proves to be unendurable, at least consider it a steppingstone to a major symphony orchestra, which would certainly be an excellent place to wait out the call to join, as the orchestras of Boston, Chicago, New York, Cleveland, and Philadelphia are called, one of the "big five."

The reason it is wise to accept whatever position is offered is because vacancies in symphony orchestras do not occur as frequently as one might believe. Examine it from this point of view. In the U.S. and Canada in 1973 there were 33 major orchestras employing 2609 musicians under regular contract. Annually emerging from our 400 accredited collegiate schools of music are enough well-trained instrumentalists who are splendidly equipped to perform a creditable job in any of the major symphonies, that perhaps fifty percent of the personnel of these orchestras would have to leave each year in order to make room for most of those qualified to replace them. Even if there were such a vast turnover, where would the displaced musicians go?

Actually, outside of the big five orchestras there is a large turnover. Many musicians, seeking different or better positions, leave each year. However, although opportunities for young players are created by so many resignations annually, the large interchange of personnel among these orchestras considerably reduces the potential openings for music graduates.

The big five, on the other hand, provide such coveted positions that yearly vacancies are exceedingly few. The New York Philharmonic, which carries 106 musicians, suffered its most sweeping change of personnel the year Artur Rodzinski became its conductor. That year, seventeen musicians were replaced.

Suppose, however, that several of our little group of music graduates managed to be placed in various orchestras about the country. What kind of weekly wage and how many weeks of employment could they reasonably count upon?

Musicians' salaries have improved tremendously over the past decade, but this has been achieved with tremendous struggle. In most cities, symphonies are in desperate financial straits, experiencing deficits in a society beset by inflation and recession. The gap between income and expenditures is constant. Musicians, determined to get the wages they deserve, have mounted strikes in recent years, even at the prestigious New York Philharmonic. A recent situation in Dallas epitomizes the sort of problems being faced by orchestras throughout the country. In March of 1974, contract negotiations with the Dallas Symphony collapsed entirely because of internal conflicts, insufficient community support and $850,000 in loans. Music director Max Rudolf resigned as did others crucial to the group's functioning. Later, some concerts were restored in order to keep the group in operation.

On the other hand, events occur that give hope and symbolize the continued determination by some in the arts to bring security and well-being to our troubled urban society. In Minneapolis, the Minnesota Orchestra played their opening 1974 concert in a new 7.2 million dollar Orchestra Hall. Their Orchestral Association raised more than $13,000 for the not yet finished modern complex.

Assuming that one of our aspiring music graduates found employment in 1973–74 with one of the orchestras outside the big five (and not including opera or ballet groups), he would have found regular season of 30–52 weeks of employment with some optional weeks, perhaps, in addition. Basic weekly pay would range from $177.45 to $305.00 and guaranteed annual wages from $4,692 to $15,860. Contract negotiations over recent years have brought benefit packages which include varying plans for hospital coverage, major medical and surgical plans, paid sick leave (ranging from 6–42 days) travel insurance, food and hotel allowances, severance pay, and numerous other benefits. Some of these symphony musicians (remember we're talking about only the 33 *major* symphonies) now make quite a decent living and enjoy benefits similar to those received by corporation employees. Most, however, must still turn to teaching and other activities related to music. Some must even rely on non-musical activities to help themselves remain at their symphony desks.

When we consider the state of the musicians who play in the big five orchestras, even though they are not paid tremendous salaries, we realize at once that they are members of full-fledged cultural institutions, accepted by their communities as cultural and social forces, and that the respect accorded them is very nearly equaled by the economic security their positions afford. For this reason, few vacancies exist. Those that occur from time to time are usually filled by men with much experience in the field. As is the case in almost all other musical areas, personal contact is of the essence. Non-musical qualities do enter the picture. Although the quality of musicianship must be extraordinarily high, personality, aggressiveness, opportunism, and intrigue are as likely to play a prominent role in securing a position, just as in other fields.

Being close to the scene of action is advantageous in knowing of a coming vacancy in making a determined bid for the position. Being appointed in this manner is no indication of political maneuvering. Nevertheless, it would be unrealistic to assume that any human enterprise can remain completely free of skulduggery.

Contract negotiations have brought significant gains to the members of the big five orchestras. The base pay in these orchestras ranges from $285 for Cleveland to $350 for the New York Philharmonic and Chicago. All five pay on the basis of a fifty-two week year including, for all but Cleveland, forty-nine days of paid vacation. (Cleveland gives a maximum of six weeks.) All but Philadelphia has a guaranteed annual wage of over $18,000 and Philadelphia's is $17,680. Boston and New York have, in addition, a guaranteed $1000 recording fee; Philadelphia's is $2000. All but Cleveland have handsome non-contributory pension plans. Boston, for example, gives a maximum of $675.00 per month and has no compulsory retirement age. This means a total of $8,100 a year. Other orchestras with comparatively good pay and benefit scales are Cincinnati, Detroit, Los Angeles, Minnesota, National, Pittsburgh, St. Louis and San Francisco.

Following are the base weekly salaries in 1973–74 for some of the other symphonies. Remember, these are among the thirty-three major groups in the U.S. and Canada; there are over 1430 others which don't pay nearly as well. San Antonio: $190; Syracuse: $138; Montreal: $245; Rochester: $255; Denver: $230; Atlanta: $243; Kansas City: $205.

The first-chair men of all orchestras customarily receive emoluments in addition to the regular minimum wage. The amount depends upon the nature of the responsibility, the reputation and comparative excellence of the player, and the ability or willingness of the orchestra to pay.

The concertmaster who is the *first* violinist of an orchestra not only plays all the solo violin passages called for in the music, but also is the leader and mentor of the string section. Occasionally, he may assist the conductor or take his place. His is a career of unusual longevity and he is also well paid. In the lesser orchestras, one may make as little as twice the minimum scale while the major orchestras pay even more. If he does some other teaching or other playing on the side, the concertmaster can have a wonderfully satisfying and lucrative career. Such is the position of Joseph Silverstein, concertmaster of the Boston Symphony Orchestra. When Mr. Silverstein joined the orchestra in 1955 he was, at the age of 23, its youngest member. In 1962 he became concertmaster and in 1971 Assistant Conductor as well. Mr. Silverstein is also soloist and first violinist of the Boston Symphony Chamber Players, which tours widely and records, first violinist of the Boston Symphony String Quartet, and a member of the Boston Symphony String Trio. He also teaches at Yale and privately.

One other extremely important post is that of contractor or personnel manager, the man in charge of hiring, firing and payroll. The contractors of the big five, except Philadelphia, are non-playing as their duties are all-consuming. The contractor is well-paid for his services, generally receiving at least double the minimum scale for his work.

Midway between the solo concert artist and the large symphony orchestra come the chamber groups and smaller ensembles. These groups, with far less personnel than symphony orchestras, can operate with much smaller budgets and therefore it would seem that the demand for such organizations would be very great. However, although many brilliant artists are members of such assemblages, only a few of them, with glittering reputations, are able to work regularly and earn good fees.

Many fine chamber orchestras are able to secure profitable bookings only several times a year. Occasionally, they may be given several successive weeks of regular concertizing, but in the aggregate their choice dates occur so sporadically that many musicians who work in this area derive the major portions of their incomes from other work, particularly from free-lance dates.

Gaining entry to one of these groups can be as difficult as getting into one of the big five symphony orchestras. Joining one of those that works less often is also difficult because in small groups the musical togetherness (both as regards their musical thinking and their precision in playing) and the unity of purpose that exists among the members is as essential an ingredient of an artistic performance as it is a bond of friendship.

As in all human relationships, friction may cause one or more members to leave the group and this, of course, will pave the way for newcomers. However, the small orchestra, with its extreme transparency, puts demands upon the players that, in most instances, exceed those made upon the players in a large symphony orchestra. For this reason, the inexperienced player has great difficulty in gaining acceptance to a well-known small ensemble, although colleges and conservatories have many miniature orchestras and string quartets that are of great value to the student who can spend some time learning the literature as a member of one of them. Such experience plus symphonic experience will give him the necessary grounding for such a group, and if, while holding down such a position as a chair in a symphony orchestra, he continues to play with high quality chamber groups (even if they are not professional), his familiarity with the idiom will keep him in readiness should a vacancy occur that he might be asked to fill.

Salaries in chamber orchestras vary tremendously. A member of a very well-known quartet may do better than a member of a big symphony orchestra, but members of less well-known quartets, woodwind groups, and larger orchestras usually will not. However, the man with whose name the group is identified should, if they are booked regularly, do very well indeed, although probably not as well as a first-rank solo concert artist.

Because of the rather limited incomes generally provided by this extremely specialized art music, and because general public acceptance is so difficult to realize, many chamber ensembles are seeking out, and are being sought out for, positions in residence at many colleges and universities. This practice is growing so rapidly that it appears to offer the most sensible form of subsidy as well as the path to the salvation of the highly skilled artists who play this priceless music.

CHAPTER IV

The Musical Theatre

During the years when vaudeville was flourishing, practically every theatre in the country had its complement of musicians. Even those theatres that did not present vaudeville employed house organists, and many theatres that had stage shows employed organists in addition to pit orchestras. As vaudeville declined, musical job opportunities eroded away until 18,000 musicians were displaced. This depression among musicians had taken place as early as 1930, a scant two years after the introduction of sound movies.

Today, to the best of my knowledge, there is but one movie house in the land that regularly employs an orchestra—Radio City Music Hall in New York City, one of the city's leading tourist attractions since it opened some *forty* years ago. There, an orchestra of symphonic proportion majestically accompanies the lavish stage presentations for which the Hall is justly famous. The orchestra's schedule includes four performances each day over a span of about nine and one-half hours. The musicians work a five day week and minimum scale brings them about $345 per week. But even this last bastion of regular theatre employment has cut down its schedule. The musicians now have a thirty-eight week season instead of the former fifty-two weeks.

The remaining musicians finding employment in the theatre serve in musical comedy, opera, and ballet productions. Musical comedy employs, by far, the greatest number of musicians in this area. Their services are required in Broadway and Off Broadway productions, road tours, summer theatre, and music tent presentations. Some cities maintain one or two theatres a large part of the year, but the most lucrative and most regular use of theatre musicians is in New York City. (This book will not explore the dramatic theatre, which, for the most part, uses no more than three or four musicians, when it uses any, to play entr'actes. Nor will it discuss circus musicians, who, in the large circuses, are hired locally as the show moves about, and, in the smaller circuses, although they are regularly employed, usually number no more than six and have to double on other jobs as well.)

The Broadway show musician not only receives the best income of theatre musicians, but enjoys great prestige and a fair degree of security. Broadway theatre musicians are among the most gifted in the land. Union regulations guarantee a musician in this job the run-of-the-show. That means that he can neither be fired nor quit his job as long as the show is running. (However, private arrangements between a contractor and a player which permit the player to leave a show that is finishing its run to join another that promises to have a long run encounter no union obstacles.)

He plays six evening performances each week plus two matinees. His minimum salary is *$290* a week. (*If he plays double instruments he receives $42 extra for the first instrument and $22 for the second.*) One musician in each orchestra is designated librarian and is paid an extra salary equivalent to the double instrument musician. Key men, such as first trumpet, first trombone, or first saxophone, usually receive an additional thirty percent over the regular pay. The same is true of the concertmaster, who must conduct the orchestra in the conductor's absence and who is most likely to inherit the role permanently should the conductor leave. Minimum scale for the conductor is seventy-five percent over the $290 base. In reality, approximately ninety percent of the conductors have their own contracts with the producers and earn considerably more. Pianists receive $290 for forty hours or less within six days. They get $26 additional if they work on Sunday and above this they are paid an hourly rate.

Recent statistics show that during the winter season from ten to thirteen musical shows run concurrently in New York's theatre district. In the summer, this number may drop as low as six or seven. Broadway shows generally employ from twenty-five to thirty-five musicians in each orchestra. Therefore, from three to four hundred musicians find employment with fair regularity in this area.

There are a few contractors, employed by theatrical producers, who hire most of the Broadway show musicians. Their positions are unofficial with no union scale for their services. They negotiate their own "deals" receiving a flat weekly fee from the producers for each show. Each theatre, however, which employs musicians must have an official contractor, different and separate from the producers'. They receive a weekly salary of $290. Actually the theatre contractors hire the men that the producers' contractors instruct them to, and they are responsible to the union for working conditions, payrolls, etc., while the producers hire their own boys to oversee and safeguard the interests of the producers.

In this area, as in almost all other musical fields, personal contact is of paramount importance in gaining one of these jobs. Being known and having one's work known to the contractor will usually be the prerequisite, although the recommendations of the conductor or of anyone of standing on the production staff usually carry sufficient weight to gain one a pit job.

When one leaves the Broadway theatre to explore Off Broadway, road company, and summer theatre productions of musical comedy, he finds that the number of musicians employed, the number of weeks of employment, and the salaries drop sharply. Some productions employ two pianists; others have full-size Broadway orchestras. Minimum wages for Off Broadway musicians are $240 weekly for eight performances or less.

The decline of the dramatic and the musical theatre all over America (read Walter Kerr's "How Not to Write a Play" for an account of this) points up the fact that most theatre employment away from New York City is sporadic and the few fairly regular theatre jobs that exist are few indeed. No other American city—not Chicago, not Boston, not Philadelphia, not San Francisco, not Los Angeles—can offer the theatrical opportunities that prevail in New York City.

The remaining musical theatre productions consist of performances of opera and ballet. The difficulty of this form of music, especially twentieth-century ballet music, is such that the players must possess the very highest skills. Large symphonic orchestras are employed, and their wage scale is similar to that of the Broadway theatre.

The same men are generally hired each season so long as the principal conductor is unchanged. Personnel, then, is determined largely by the preferences of the conductor. New conductors bring their favorite players with them, as a rule.

Ballet seasons are notably short, as are most opera seasons. The principal exception to this is the Metropolitan Opera Company of New York whose winter season of 1974–75 was thirty weeks followed by a spring tour during May and June.

Here are a few examples of the lengths of ballet and opera seasons for the same year: San Francisco Opera, September 13—December 1; Opera Society of Washington, four weeks; Chicago Lyric Opera, September 20—December 14 (three to five performances per week); Opera Company of Boston, three performances each month for February, April, May, June plus two month tour; Baltimore Opera Company, three performances each month in October, November, February, April plus one or two month tour; Kansas City Opera, September 24—October 26; New York City Opera, August 28—November 10 and February 20—April 27; Philadelphia Lyric Opera, two performances in November, one in February, two in March and two in May; San Diego Opera, three performances each month for October and April; Joffrey Ballet, four weeks in March (eight performances a week); New York City Ballet, two months (eight performances a week).

The concert musician whose work is chiefly in the ballet and opera field must regard his work as free-lance. There are a few exceptions, most notably those musicians in the Metropolitan Opera Orchestra. In 1972–73, the members of this orchestra were paid a basic weekly wage of $345 for a fifty-one week year and had a guaranteed annual wage of $17,595. As we have seen, most ballet, opera, and symphony musicians have short regular seasons and make themselves available for extra opera and ballet performances when it is possible. The musician who plays most of the events that occur in his city can manage, possibly, to scrape together a living, but unless he teaches or engages in some other pursuit, he will have no easy time of it. Touring companies from the large cities deprive local musicians of some work, but many touring companies take only a few key men on the road and make up the rest of the orchestra with local talent.

As in most other areas, New York City offers the greatest opportunities for employment in the ballet-opera area. Ballet and opera producers are not averse to realizing a profit, but their productions, entailing the employment of large orchestras, are very expensive. Rarely can expenses be cut substantially without damaging the artistic quality of the production. Losses are usually underwritten by private individuals. Therefore, unhappily for the musicians involved, long seasons characterized by tremendous financial loss are prohibitive.

Musical comedy, on the other hand, designed primarily to make money, keeps its doors open so long as it is profitable. When a show loses money, it closes. The musical comedy musician, who enjoys much more security than his artistic brother in the ballet and opera field, must still face two very real dangers. First, since few productions are initiated in summer, should a show in which he is working close in mid-spring, he is apt to be caught without a show until early, or even late, fall. The other danger is that playing the same music eight performances each week for any protracted period of time can dull his sensitivities to music and wreak havoc with his enthusiasm.

A tremendous advantage of working in the musical theatre (except Radio City Music Hall) is that there is ample time during a number of weekdays for other pursuits such as teaching or free-lance recording and transcription dates. Some theatre musicians study and learn non-musical pursuits. Some have become daytime real-estate brokers, insurance men, stockbrokers, and mutual-fund salesmen, to mention but a few possibilities.

Arrangers and copyists for the musical theatre are well paid for their work. This is an exceptionally difficult area in which to gain a foothold, for, by and large, the same arrangers (orchestrators) and copyists get the Broadway assignments, show after show. Some arrangers, such as Robert Russell Bennett, whose contributions to the success of a production are so great, may even be given a percentage of the show's profits. Entry may eventually be gained as a result of a long and outstanding record in other areas, coupled with a little luck.

It is not quite so difficult to become a conductor of a Broadway show, although violinists and pianists seem to have the greatest opportunities in this direction. This is because concertmasters are in a position to gain the experience and are the most logical to succeed to the job in the event that the conductor leaves. It takes only a few such credits for a producer to entrust the musical direction to such a man. Pianists, too, because of their complete familiarity with the score and because of the close contact they are able to maintain with production people (the result of their roles as rehearsal-pianists), frequently get a chance to become conductors. The experience a musician gains from conducting summer stock, where he is required to conduct a different show every week, can stand him in good stead if he has his eye on a conductor's post in the Broadway theatre.

To sum up, the picture of the musical theatre and the musical theatre musician, from a national point of view, is anything but bright. However, although there is tremendous room for improvement, the New York situation is better than tolerable. There, several hundred musicians regularly derive fairly good incomes from this source.

CHAPTER V

The Free-Lance Musician

There is a category of musicians that, in New York and Los Angeles, rises to a position of great importance in the music field. It is of less importance in other cities, but most fair-sized cities have enough of this kind of work to sustain at least some musicians. This category is that of the free-lance musician.

Here we will explore briefly the nature of the free-lance music field and free-lance musicians, while several of the following chapters will examine, in more detail, the various areas that make up the classification.

The free-lance musician is one who works on single engagements. He may accept this sort of employment in addition to a regular, steady job, as for example, when the musician who plays every night in a club or hotel accepts single dates during the day. Musicians who are regularly engaged in other industries and who accept weekend playing jobs are free-lance musicians. Theatre musicians who can squeeze in such dates in their free hours are also part of the free-lance scene.

Outside of the fees paid to celebrity musicians, the rates in the free-lance field are higher than anywhere else in music. For this reason, free-lance dates provide a wonderful supplement to the income earned from a regular job. Of course, the benefits to the individual are dependent on the number of such dates he can snag.

The field generally covers such single engagements as recording dates (making commercial phonograph records), transcriptions (recording "jingles," TV spot music backgrounds, or adding to the libraries of such music-supplying services as Muzak), film dates that provide the music backgrounds for movie theatre films or filmed or taped television programs. It includes such work as club dates or regular, weekly live television or radio shows that do not employ staff musicians but go to the outside to employ free-lance musicians on a single engagement basis (one show and rehearsal per week). It may include three or four weeks at the Waldorf to help augment the band for some performer who requires a larger orchestra than the house normally provides. This last falls technically under the heading of steady work, but because it is of such a temporary nature, it seems much more logical to include it in the field of free-lance work, especially since the men filling such positions are usually recruited from the outside.

Of the above-mentioned areas, those jobs whose specific purpose is to provide music for mass audiences (as by mass production of recordings, or supplying radio and TV stations all over the country with jingles, or through network facilities releasing recorded or live programs to the public at large) are termed "studio" jobs. This is by all odds the most lucrative work in the free-lance field.

In New York and in Los Angeles a small segment of studio men finds itself in a most enviable position. These men are able to devote themselves almost exclusively to this kind of work, and, in return, this select little group pretty much monopolizes the field. These men regularly earn from $20,000 per year on up to six figures. A typically busy player who does studio work exclusively may consistently earn from $30,000 to $40,000 per year. The upper limits of the studio side man's income are determined by the number of hours he is physically able to work each day.

Some of the men in this field are contractors, conductors, or arrangers. If they are busy enough, they earn considerably more than the players and so find themselves in the top income bracket of free-lance musicians. Other players add substantially to their incomes by contracting, conducting, or arranging (or performing all three functions) as often as such opportunities present themselves.

Many of the men in the free-lance field are truly artists, yet rarely is anything more than competent musical craftsmanship demanded of them. Studio musicians especially are among the most gifted in the world, but despite the fact that they are usually called upon to play nothing but third-rate inanities, few contractors or leaders are disposed to settle for anyone but the very best.

The free-lance field has its ups and downs; there are periods of tremendous activity followed by periods of relative barrenness. Therefore, for many free-lance musicians, weekly income rarely becomes stabilized. Those musicians who are most in demand, being first call with many contractors and leaders, rarely feel the pinch when business is slow, but those who normally play the dates turned down by the first-call men suffer immediately if there is a letdown in activity.

One of the hazards of free-lance work lies in working for one or two contractors or leaders exclusively. Should these leaders or contractors lose their work, move away, or in some other manner become unable to employ the men who have grown dependent upon them, their musicians are in danger of being left high and dry with no ready work available. (It is not the practice of leaders and contractors suddenly to drop men whose work has been quite satisfactory merely to make room for musicians who have been regularly employed by other people but have unexpectedly become available.)

It is not considered a wise practice to refuse to accept a date for personal reasons, although some men, especially if they are very busy with recordings and transcriptions from Mondays through Fridays, habitually keep their weekends free from work. The only acceptable reasons for turning down dates are illness or a previous commitment, and contractors are not happy about either excuse. In fact, many contractors feel that the men they consistently call first have an obligation to be available. For some contractors it does not take too many replies of "Sorry, I'm busy at that time" before they stop calling and seek out someone to take his place.

Two other drawbacks to free-lance work are conflicts and no vacations. The bane of any musician who depends upon single dates for a living is to be called for dates whose times mutually overlap. The pity, of course, is that conflicts seem to occur most often when the musician is undergoing a slow period. Some musicians, however, manage to take advantage of periods of lessened activity to get away for short vacations, because the nature of free-lance work, just as in the case of doctors and free-lance artists and writers, precludes the possibility of paid vacations.

Musicians whose work consists of single engagements are virtual slaves of the telephone, their lifeline to work. (Club date employment can also be procured on the union exchange floor.) Many such musicians employ telephone message services, so that calls that come in when no one is at home can be relayed to them. Since these men have no way of knowing when a call or a date is forthcoming, and because there are no rules about being needed on very short notice, long-range social plans frequently are impossible. Further, it is not at all unusual for a long-anticipated social or recreational appointment to be cancelled at the last moment. (This writer well recalls one season when he had purchased theatre tickets well in advance, planning to attend once a week for the entire winter. Sudden illness of the children or a last-minute call for a date prevented our seeing all but three or four productions during the entire season and caused us to give away most of the tickets that had been ordered so many months before—tickets for performances we had looked forward to with such eagerness.)

The free-lance field, despite its drawbacks, is one of the most exciting areas in which to work. The lack of regularity and sameness prevent the boredom of most jobs from taking hold. One's work is here, there, anywhere. The varied environment is matched by the diverse personalities with whom one comes in contact. The free-lance musician works for many different conductors in the course of his musical life and plays an integral role in the performance of dozens of artists, stars, and celebrities, many of whom he comes to know intimately. Most fascinating of all for the free-lance musician is the complete absence of foreknowledge concerning career opportunities or situations that may lie around the corner just waiting for tomorrow or next week to be confronted. And for all this the free-lance musician is quite well paid; indeed, a busy career in this field can help to amass a small fortune for a prudent man.

CHAPTER VI

Club Dates

The club date field is probably the biggest single field for musicians in the entire music business. This is because no main centers provide the music for club dates for the rest of the country. Local musicians play these dates most frequently, and fully 95 percent of all musicians whose work is not devoted to the concert field play at least some club dates in their lives; and undoubtedly many of those in the concert field play club dates occasionally.

Club dates are all those single engagements that are not in the classification of recordings, transcriptions, film dates, or radio and television broadcasts and, as such, fall under the general heading of free-lance work. In Boston, club dates are referred to as "general business," while Californians call them "casuals."

Club dates can be anything from agricultural shows to wedding ceremonies. The designation covers such engagements as outings, band or orchestra concerts, athletic games, bar mitzvahs, fairs, private parties, dances, banquets, confirmations, conventions, dinners, exhibitions, fashion shows, fiestas, luncheons, breakfasts, religious services, minstrel shows, parades, rodeos, skating rinks, strawberry festivals, and others. Most club dates are dances of one kind or another, and some require a show to be played during the engagement. Country club dances, organization affairs, banquets, or receptions given by individuals are high on the list of club date activities.

Some club dates use "set" bands—that is, regularly organized groups in which the same men always work together (barring occasional personnel changes), as is the case with regularly organized name dance bands. But most club dates use what are termed "pick-up" bands. That is to say that the leader or whoever is responsible for engaging personnel, after first having decided what his requirements are, selects the men he wants from a large pool of available musicians. The desired musicians are then called and if they are not already committed for the night or nights in question, they are hired. Those men who, because of some previous commitment, are unable to accept are replaced by other musicians from the lists that every leader or club date office possesses. This does not mean that many musicians will not find themselves working side by side with the same men, week after week or night after night, since all leaders and contractors have their favorites and try to engage them as far ahead as possible to be sure of having them. Nevertheless, despite the regularity with which these men work together, they do not constitute set bands, but are, because of the manner in which they are engaged, pick-up bands.

There is a variety of special skills and talents required of club date musicians, and the demands of individual engagements will determine which special talents or qualities are necessary. Some musicians have cultivated certain qualities into such highly developed skills that they have come to be known as specialists, and the demand for their services for particular kinds of work is very great.

The first requirement of the club date musician, as it is of every type of orchestral player, is a well-developed skill in ensemble playing. But the club date field differs most from all others in that it is largely a memory field. Since music is rarely brought to or used at engagements that have dancing and since the rapid transition from one tune to another without plan, or the necessity to play requests as they are made, precludes the searching out of individual song sheets or orchestrations from a book full of them, the club date musician is required to "know the tunes." This means that the musician has to know from memory all or most of the two thousand or so tunes most commonly played and requested and the keys in which they are usually played. Besides, he must keep abreast of the current popular hits as well as the better known tunes from current Broadway shows and the movies. Since music of the 70's has been essentially trendless, his repetoire must encompass music of many styles including hard and soft rock tunes, country, western, soul, ballads and nostalgic returns to the 30's and 40's. Add to this a smattering of folk dances and folk tunes of many lands as well as the popular favorites of Jewish, Greek, Italian, Polish, and other ethnic groups and you will see that the club date musician must have at his command a rather impressive storehouse of musical material.

Naturally, the metropolitan club date musician is expected to be familiar with a greater variety of music than the one-string fiddler who plays barn dances in Peeled Chestnut, Tennessee, but, on the other hand, the latter must know a good many more folk dances, folk tunes, and square dance material than the musician in the big city. The breadth and depth of the club date musician's repertoire are dictated by the degree of sophistication of his audiences and by the extent to which the population in his geographical area is ethnically varied. The musician in New York or Chicago has to know and play a much greater variety of tunes than the musician in the rural area, especially if that rural area lacks the flavor of the melting pot.

Few musicians can remember every single tune that may be requested, but usually if one musician in the group does not remember some particular song, another one will, so that almost anything requested can be played. The pianist, of course, is expected to know every song imaginable or be well able to fake it, and the other musicians who do not remember a song will usually be able to fake the tune by the time the beginning of the chorus comes around a second time.

There is nothing faked about the ability to fake. Musical faking is a skill of the highest order. It requires a highly trained ear and a tremendously retentive tonal memory. Suppose, for example, that you are the pianist on a club date and a tune is requested that only a trumpet players knows. He tells you the key in which he will play it and you modulate, leading him to that key. If the tune is vaguely familiar to you, you will have a general idea of its shape and, possibly, of its over-all harmonization. If it is totally unfamiliar to you, you will not know its construction, so you will have to feel your way around and seek out the harmonic patterns. If the harmonies are simple, this presents no problem, but when the tune is complicated and there are obscure modulations in the song, faking becomes much more difficult.

As the tune is being played, you must memorize it while determining which harmonies sound best. At the same time, you must analyze what was wrong when the harmonies did not seem to fit and how to correct them so that by the time any phrase is repeated you will not only have learned the melody but will have discovered which harmonic patterns seem correct. Since most tunes conform to an AABA form, by the time you have reached the B section, you have learned three-fourths of the tune and, by the second chorus, you will have learned that section as well. Tunes that do not conform to this shape may be more elusive, but all songs have sections that repeat, if not in their entirety at least in part, and you will alert yourself to those guideposts, phrases that repeat, learning the tune and its harmonies as you go, while keeping track of its general structure. If some of the other musicians join in and fake some harmonies, listen to them and be guided by what they play. They will certainly be listening to you as a means of grasping the harmonies, and this kind of interdependency can result in a most satisfactory rendition.

The remarkable accuracy with which a musician possessing a good ear can fake a tune is really shocking. Developing a good ear and the ability to fake is a worthwhile skill in any musician, but it is definitely an attribute of the club date player.

Years ago, the only requirement for the club date player was that he know the tunes. It mattered not how poor was his harmonic sense or how inferior was the quality of his tone. It did not mean a thing that he possessed but limited technical skill, and his failure to play in tune seemed not to offend anyone. Today, the picture is changed considerably. The quality of playing on club dates is continually improving, and it is already at a respectable level in a good many instances, at a really high level in others.

It is not unusual to hear club date musicians play with marvelous conception and flawless intonation. There are many trumpet players, trombonists and saxophonists who can fake second, third, or fourth harmony parts so accurately that brass and reed sections sound as if they are reading brilliant arrangements. Unquestionably, the fact that many young musicians with excellent jazz backgrounds have filtered into the club date field has been, to a great degree, responsible for raising the standards of musicianship among the club daters.

It is true that for many club dates the ability to read well is inconsequential since no music is used. As stated before, however, many club dates require that show as well as dance music be played. Although it is not uncommon for acts to come in without music, expecting a "talk-over" rehearsal and a faked performance by the orchestra with impromptu transposition for singers, faked shows are the exception rather than the rule. Most commonly, when there is a show to be played, a regular rehearsal is scheduled before the engagement begins. Since show music may consist of anything from simple blues and pop songs on through operatic arias and symphonic excerpts to ballet sequences, the musicians must be fluent sight-readers and adept at following a conductor. Besides, these men never know when a performer will suddenly turn to the orchestra, mention the name of some obscure tune, a key, the fact that he wants a four-bar introduction and one and a half choruses, stomp his foot, and away you go.

Of course, all club date musicians cannot do all these things well, but every year more and more of them are gaining this kind of versatility. However, the specialists generally perform their special functions better than those who generalize.

When a club date consists of a ballet, a symphony concert, or an opera, a pick-up orchestra consisting of men with special skill and experience in this direction is chosen.

If a club date consists of a particularly difficult show or the show outweighs the dance music in importance, the best show musicians are employed, and if they are not familiar with all the tunes to be played from memory, a music library consisting of stock and/or special arrangements is brought in from which they can read the dance music. Some club date dance bands use music almost exclusively, but this is much less common than playing without music.

Some musicians make a specialty of weddings and know best how to please wedding guests. Besides learning the traditional and sacred wedding songs, they are very familiar with the appropriate songs of foreign derivation. For example, if it is a Greek wedding, they know enough popular Greek songs to play all night. The same is true if the wedding is Italian or Armenian or what have you.

Other musicians become specialists in gypsy music or Hungarian or Russian music. There are thousands of such tunes and this knowledge is gained only through years of being steeped in one particular element. Many of these musicians are foreign born and brought much of this knowledge of the literature with them to this country when they immigrated. But although much club date music is still poorly played, the current crop of American-born musicians has done much to raise the standards of club date music, and these musicians are increasingly extending their versatility to all areas of the field.

Is there a career to be had in club dates? Yes. Is the field hard to enter? Yes. All musical fields are hard to enter, but the club date field does not keep its doors shut as tightly as other fields do. Why do so many jazz musicians come into the club date field? Because it is generally more lucrative than the jazz field unless they are connected with a name group. Don't musicians from other fields play club dates? Yes. A number of studio and recording musicians play club dates to supplement their income or to keep a finger in the field. But there is a danger in club dates to the studio musician. Few of them know all the tunes, and in spite of tremendous instrumental skill one can easily step all over one's reputation in the first five minutes of a job. Result: the other musicians look down upon this high and mighty visitor and pin a new label on him—"He does not know all the tunes."

Are they this unkind to musicians who do not come from studio work? It is not a question of unkindness. The nature of the business demands that the musician be able to play instantly whatever the leader calls out. This is a necessity regardless of where the newcomer is from. There may be some hostility to the studio musician fostered by an unconscious jealousy, but generally the experienced club date musicians try to guide newcomers and help make their way a little easier if they can. Unfortunately, it is only the occasional leader or contractor who can be charged with such forbearance.

How does one get into the club date field? There are three principal ways of getting to play club dates and all three should be used.

There are union halls all over the country where members gather to chat, to while away time, and to engage men or to be engaged for club dates. In New York City the union headquarters has what is called an exchange floor, which is open Monday, Wednesday, and Friday until three in the afternoon. Members gather there for the sole purpose of booking and being booked, and there is a frightening amount of activity on the New York exchange floor.

This is really a sight to behold—several thousand members milling about like people gathered on a subway platform during the rush hour; the room filled with smoke and thousands of loud voices blending into a tumultuous cacophony, all of which is merely the background to a blaring loudspeaker that pierces your eardrums every few seconds, paging one member or another, or seeking someone for a Saturday night job or a week out of town. Here gather the fat and the lean, the well-fed and the hungry, the old and the young, the forlorn and the hopeful, each attempting vainly to maintain a facade of bravado while the pangs of anxiety gnaw at his innards. No one really succeeds in concealing his fears, but each of his fellows is too preoccupied with his own problems ever to recognize, as he looks about him, that all wear the same mask—the expression of the eyes, the twist of the smiles, the lines of the foreheads are living reflections of his own face. Each, try though he might to hide it, wears the tag of uncertainty.

Yes, you must, above all else, go up to the union hall and keep your eyes and ears open. Engage people in conversation, make friends, and listen to the announcements that are being made. If you hear a call for a job you can do, go up and volunteer for it. Ask around concerning the leaders who need someone for the weekend. If you hear of someone, try to meet him or, failing to find him, have him paged. Don't be discouraged by all of those you see at the union who are also looking for work. There are jobs to be had and the union floor is an ideal place for leader and side man to get together.

Sooner or later you will wind up with your first date and your new career will have been launched.

The second method for obtaining club date jobs is to find out the names and addresses of the leading club date offices in town and to present yourself with a request to meet the leader. If he is not in, do not loiter and do not make a pest of yourself. Plan to come back again and again until you do meet him. After you have been back several times, you will be recognized, and if your manner has been pleasant, it will be that much easier to meet the boss. When you do meet him, tell him what you play and what, if any, professional experience you have had. No résumé is necessary or even desired and it is unlikely that you will be auditioned. Your name, instrument, and phone number is probably all the information you will be asked to leave.

You probably will not get a job from any of these offices right away, so the best plan would then be to stop in regularly to let them know you are still around and available. Your chance will come some very busy weekend when the office has booked all its regular men on jobs and still has to find personnel for other jobs. Then they go through the lists of names of those whom they do not use regularly. These are the musicians they call when they are loaded with work and are stuck for men to fill the jobs. Since busy weekends for them are busy weekends for other offices and since many of their second- and third-string men will already have been hired by other offices, they will be forced to engage some men not used previously, and your call will come.

The third method is the word-of-mouth method and is, in a way, dependent upon the other two methods. It means making friends with other musicians and doing a creditable job when you get a chance to work. Thus, word will get around of your dependability, availability, and qualifications. A good reputation does much to bring work to a musician and with such a reputation a word of recommendation from a friend can frequently bring dates that otherwise might not have been forthcoming.

The following instruments are the ones most frequently used on club dates, especially in small combinations, which are booked in far greater numbers than large combinations. (Small combinations are usually three to seven men in size, while the larger groups generally employ ten or twelve men and rarely use more than twenty-five or thirty.) Almost all club dates use piano, but most club date pianists must double on accordion. This gives the unit flexibility in that it can stroll among the audience when desired, or even play a date in a room that boasts no piano. Trumpet is frequently used and the trumpeter is not required to double on another instrument, although some play mellophone or a similar brass instrument. Trombone is used occasionally but not as frequently as trumpet. Saxophone is used almost always and saxophonists are required to double on clarinet. However, since many saxophonists come from studio work or have designs on that type of work, it is common for them to double on other wood-wind instruments, and flute makes a valuable double. Any additional wood-wind doubles besides clarinet are definite plus values to the club date reed player. Violin is frequently called for, but there is little demand for viola or 'cello. There is but little demand for guitar on club dates, and even larger bands frequently dispense with it, although a good guitarist can be a tremendous asset to a small group. String bass is used very frequently, but some small groups get along without it despite its tremendous importance both as a rhythm instrument and as a means of giving a solid musical bottom to the aggregate sound. No double is required of bassists. Drummers are only rarely omitted from club date bands, especially since percussion sounds are needed to give Latin American music its characteristic color. No mallet doubles are required of club date drummers, but occasionally tympani must be played if there is a show. Nevertheless, drummers carry a goodly assortment of Latin percussion instruments, some of which, like maracas and claves, can be played by other side men, besides their regular assortment of cymbals and drums. Vibraphones may occasionally be used on club dates, but, despite its increasing popularity, most club date leaders prefer the above-mentioned instruments. There is little or no call for any other instruments on club dates.

An asset to any club date musician is his ability to sing. The musician who can stand up and sing ten or twelve tunes during the night will frequently be hired in preference to musicians who do not sing. Often these singing musicians display little vocal talent, their gifts consisting of a knowledge of melody and lyrics and a colossal nerve. I have run across several "singing bass players" whose instrumental skill was woefully undistinguished and whose attempts at vocalising were an affront to discriminating ears. Yet, these men work and work consistently. The man who combines superior instrumental skill with a solid vocal talent is, of course, difficult to come by, but anyone who possesses such skills and knows the tunes should experience little difficulty in getting work and should soon find considerable demand for his services in all types of dance work. However, although singing can prove of inestimable advantage to club date musicians, the fact remains that most of them get along quite well without ever singing a note.

In estimating the potential income of the club date musician, we run into many variables. Wage scales vary from one city to another. Even within the confines of a given city, scales are dependent upon the kind of engagement, the class of engagement (which depends upon where it is held, each specific location or room being given an arbitrary classification by the musicians' union), whether it is a morning, afternoon, or evening engagement; whether there is a show and/or rehearsal in connection with the engagement; and whether or not there are overtime charges. And, of course, the musician's income is dependent upon how many of these engagements he plays.

The rates in New York City, probably among the highest in the country, provide us with a rough evaluation of what the club date player may hope for, particularly if he should seek work there, and especially since this kind of work is most plentiful in New York.

The average class "A" club date in New York and vicinity pays from $39 to $58 per job for the side man. Rehearsal for a show pays him at the rate of $10.50 per hour with a minimum of two hours. Overtime will give him $13.00 per hour from Sunday to Friday and $14.50 on Saturday. This is for non-continuous engagements. For continuous engagements—that is where there is less than ten minutes between sets or where the sets exceed twenty minutes in length—the comparable rates are $48–$70 for a side man and overtimes of $17 for Sunday to Friday and $18.50 for Saturday nights. Included in these scale rates are Pension Fund contributions.

There are such additional charges as cartage (for heavy instruments) and mileage for dates beyond the city limits. Every engagement must have a leader or leader-designate present at the date. He receives double the prevailing scale plus eight percent for overtime and rehearsals.

The above is not intended to be a complete breakdown of the New York City price scale, but is intended to give a fair picture of what the average kind of club date work can pay. There are many New York musicians who, by regularly playing Friday night, Saturday afternoon, Saturday night, and Sunday afternoon engagements, secure for themselves a steady weekly minimum income of about $300. If they also work more or less regularly on Wednesday and Sunday nights, they may bring their minimum weekly average up by about $100, and in very busy times, by filling most of the rest of week, they can earn as much as, or even more than, $700 a week.

Tips and gratuities can add significantly to earnings, but it is impossible to predict what the income from tips will amount to. Obviously, the more often a man works the more likely he is to receive tips. Some men regularly get from $35–$60 a week or more just from this source. The leaders of such dates generally earn twice as much as the side men, as explained before.

There is a fair amount of solo club date work for pianist-accordionists, and they usually earn sizable amounts above the scale. Remember, too, that the small combination, having fewer musicians to divide up tips, offers the musician a greater opportunity to take home more money than the larger orchestra. Similarly, the solo musician, having to split his tips with no one, has the best chance of all to regard this as a potent source of additional income.

The club date musician with an eye to the future, a bit of salesmanship, and a modicum of business acumen can increase his income potential many times by opening his own office and booking his own dates. Often all that is required to get the ball rolling is one contact—a friend on the entertainment committee of a country club, a neighbor about to give a wedding reception, or the manager of a local catering establishment. (One word of caution in this matter: It is absolutely taboo when playing an engagement for someone else, upon being questioned by a guest regarding availability for a future date, to refer him to anyone but the leader on that particular date, and that leader must, in turn, refer the guest to the office that employed him. It is absolutely forbidden to solicit work for anyone except the leader who hired you or for whom you are working. All potential work accruing from a particular date is to be recommended to the leader whose account the particular date is. This is accepted practice and is the manner in which club date booking offices grow.)

By advertising, by calling on potential accounts, and by word of mouth, the individual can build up a fair-sized annual business, which can dwarf his income as a side man. While it is true that there are a few giants in the field whose positions could scarcely be challenged, there are dozens upon dozens of smaller offices in the New York area that prosper and grow year after year, and the same must be true, in lesser degree, of course, in the larger metropolitan areas throughout the country.

Two things worth remembering before we go on to another field bear telling at this point. (1) Club date musicians are the work horses of the music business. Their work is hard physical labor—perhaps not as demanding as some fields of heavy labor, but certainly more fatiguing than any other kind of musical activity, with the possible exception of parade bands. It never fails to amaze me that so many club date musicians bear up well under the strain of playing six to ten dates a week month after month and year after year. It takes a tremendous amount of stamina to do this, and obviously those whose staying powers are not up to the demands of club work soon exclude themselves from much of this area and seek out less laborious fields. (2) The same qualities of personal magnetism and enthusiasm that vault concert artists into a lasting place in the public's eye can prove to be of great value to the club date musician who aspires to become a leader and to manage his own office.

Generally, the club date field can provide the musician with a fairly regular income—even with one that, judged by musicians' standards, is fairly lucrative. While it is rarely artistically rewarding, the club date field can be the basis for a useful and long-lived career to the musician who can bear to satisfy his artistic hunger elsewhere. In addition, club dates can be the source of much additional income to those who regularly pursue careers in other fields, musical or otherwise.

CHAPTER VII

Phonograph Records

There are literally thousands of recording companies in the United States. Most of them actively record, while the rest purchase "master" tapes from other companies or from individuals and manufacture records from them to be distributed to the market. Some maintain their own recording studios and equipment, and others rent the facilities they need. Although few recording companies process their own tapes and manufacture their own records, others assign this work either to recording companies who have such facilities or to outside firms whose specialty is record manufacture. (Manufacture, in this context, means to "press" the grooves into the record material, itself.) The phonograph record industry is big business, and hit records make enormous profits.

The recording industry today dominates the popular-music publishing business and the radio industry. It is the one medium in which success brings opportunities in other media. It is a medium that terms all recording personalities "artists," and it is the one medium that, above all others, equates money with merit. The recording industry is one of the mainstays of the free-lance musician, and it is of great importance to organized symphonic groups, dance bands, combos, and singing groups, since it provides considerable additional income.

With organized groups, the standard of musicianship required varies with the individual group, but for the free-lance musician, called upon as he is to play on a great variety of recording engagements, the same highly developed skills that prevail in other areas of studio work are demanded. However, despite a fair amount of over-lapping, musicians in this field are apt to be categorized. Common categories are concert (classical, if you will), Latin American, jazz, rock and roll, and light opera and musical comedy.

The two principal units of merchandising are singles and LPs. Singles are seven-inch records to be played at forty-five revolutions per minute, and contain one composition on each face. It is unusual to find that the length of any single side exceeds three minutes, and generally a disc jockey will refuse to play it if it exceeds two minutes thirty seconds. LPs are twelve-inch micro-groove discs usually con-taining no more than fifteen to seventeen minutes on each side, although some have as much as twenty-two minutes of recorded ma-terial per side. If the LPs are in the pop field, they generally in-corporate six compositions to a side. If they are in the concert field, the length of the works recorded will determine how much of each composition will be allotted to each side or, if the works are short, how many works will be pressed on each side.

Although New York City and Los Angeles are the main recording centers in the United States, recording companies can record wher-ever it is desired. Every large city and most fair-sized cities have recording firms. Some operate sporadically, others regularly. As some withdraw from the field more enter. All who use union musicians and union singers are technically bound by the same labor agreements and are committed to pay identical wage scales.

The unit time of a recording session is three hours. Musicians are allowed to record no more than four three-minute pop compositions in three hours. (Additional compositions recorded within three hours are paid for at the rate of one-half hour's overtime charges per addi-tional composition.) For recording an LP, regardless of how quickly it may have been recorded, no less than the price of three basic re-cording dates may be paid. Recording of concert music is paid for similarly as far as the basic three-hour date and overtime is con-cerned, but the numbers of composition allowed and their playing time differ from the schedule in pop records.

The current rate is $100 for three hours plus $9.00 given to the pension fund. (This price which is considered exorbitant by recording companies, has fostered the practice of recording in Europe where costs are significantly lower.) Overtime may be broken down into half-hour segments so that one and a half hours of overtime costs the same as the basic three-hour date. Minimum scale for conductors is double that of the players. The contractor receives the same fee as the player and double if he also plays on the engagement.

In the recording field, as in TV films, the arranger is often also the conductor. Although he may accept a single combined fee, provided it is not less than minimum scale for both functions, more frequently he is paid two separate fees—one for his arrangements and the other for conducting.

Arranger-conductors and conductors who do not arrange are often signed to contracts limiting their recording services to one recording company only. Such men may be used to conduct all or most of the dates in one or more departments of the recording company. Large recording companies may have separate departments for classical, children's, educational, jazz, pop, Latin American, rock and roll, country, and western and hillbilly records, or several departments may be grouped under one heading to reduce the total number of departments to three or four.

In other cases, conductors under contract are brought into the control room to help produce the recording sessions. There they help the engineers achieve optimum musical balances; they make sure that the total time of each recording is satisfactory; they check for clarity and correctness of the lyrics (if there is singing on the record); they suggest deleting or changing orchestral passages that obscure a word or two; they listen for good intonation; they decide on how much echo should be used; and they discharge a host of other chores requiring careful listening, wide experience in the recording field, and sound judgment.

This writer is not conversant with the methods of paying house conductors and conductor-producers, but the chances are that such men receive yearly retainers in addition to fees paid for participation in recording sessions. Whether the retainer is or is not charged against the fees earned, it seems clear that such house men, if the company records often enough, can earn handsome salaries. (Even a house conductor or conductor-arranger is not permitted to work for less money than the minimum union scales.)

One other category of positions with recording companies needs to be examined because a fair number of musicians occupies it, although the majority of such positions is filled by non-musicians. This is the category of A. and R. man. A. and R. means artists and repertoire. A different A. and R. man works in each department of the larger recording companies. The A. and R. man's responsibilities are many. For one thing, he must choose the material to be recorded. This alone is a full-time job, and since the A. and R. man's office is always swamped with material begging to be recorded, it would require the wisdom of Solomon to be right more often than wrong.

Usually musical material that is chosen to be recorded appears to be particularly well suited to some individual "artist" under contract to the recording company. If the material is chosen simply because of its appeal to the A. and R. man, it is his responsibility to decide which artist will perform it. In any event, he decides who will record what. Further, he is instrumental in bringing new artists to a recording company and cutting loose those he finds undesirable.

The A. and R. man is given a certain annual or semiannual budget to work with, and it is his responsibility to apportion that budget among the sessions he plans to do. A series of overtime dates, if no provision was made for them in the A. and R. man's planning, could so consume his budget that it would prevent several projected recording sessions from taking place.

Further, the A. and R. man is responsible for producing the recording session. If he has assistant and co-producers to help him, all well and good, but if not, the complete job of producing the "master" tapes falls on his shoulders.

Finally, the responsibility for record sales is his. It is not that he is accountable for promotion, distribution, or art work. Simply stated, if his department shows a profit, he is successful. If he is lucky enough to have a series of hits, he becomes a hero. On the other hand, deficits are not tolerated. A series of mistakes (errors in judging the buying habits of a fickle public) is the surest way for him to get his walking papers.

The salaries of A. and R. men vary greatly. Success can bring substantial raises, and with continued success, there is virtually no ceiling on possible income.

The skills and attitudes of the free-lance players, the conductors, and the arrangers who work in the recording field are self-evident. High qualities of musicianship and instrumental skill are taken for granted. The ability to sight read rapidly and accurately are indispensable, since there is no pre-session rehearsal period. Rehearsal and recording take place on the date itself, and there is never time to spare for deficient readers to learn parts that a facile reader would be able to handle instantaneously. Specific talents and experience are channeled into specific musical areas.

This is not quite so of the A. and R. man. His concern is the specific market for which he is aiming. He must know what kinds of things this market has bought in the past, and, without consulting a crystal ball, he must be able to predict with reasonable accuracy what the public's buying habits are apt to be in the future.

It is not enough for the classical A. and R. man to be a real authority in his field, anxious to bring to the world of record lovers the beauties of some long-neglected works or to wish to acquaint them with the charms of some unknown composers. His own musical scholarship plays but a small role in the exercise of his responsibilities. Like all other A. and R. men, he chooses material and artists with one eye on the cash register. For him, conservatism is the best approach. He knows that well-known, well-loved works, well recorded by reputable artists and orchestras, are investments that will bring his company revenue for years to come.

While exercising prudence, he can record a lesser known or an unknown work occasionally, but he must judge what kind of works they should be coupled with. Should a bright idea strike him, he must be certain to execute it in such a manner to avoid offending the sensibilities of those who may be devoted to artists and works of his company. Signing up new young artists may be a bold stroke leading to brilliant results, or it may boomerang and cause disaster. Such are the subtleties of judgment the classical A. and R. man is called upon to make.

The one recording area that overshadows all others, because of the vastness of its potential sales, is that of rock and roll and kindred fields of country and western, hillbilly, gospel, folk songs and, more recently, conventional romantic ballads (known to the recording industry as M.O.R.'s or Middle of the Road music). This area has dominated the recording industry for several years and it bids fair to continue. Vast profits have been made here; many men have become rich and powerful through it; many with a few dollars to invest and a desire to get rich quickly are lured into it; countless fools have lost heavily because of inexperience and an inability to comprehend the magnitude of the risks involved. Several large companies have supported all their other departments with profits from rock and roll. Some have built up their catalogues and prestige in their classical and educational departments with money that otherwise would have disappeared in the form of taxes—and all made possible by profits from rock and roll.

The rock-and-roll A. and R. man's job is the most sensitive in the recording company, because it is the most fiscal. Whether the company prospers or declines rests in his hands.

One of the most difficult things for the well-trained musician is to shed his musical instinct and knowledge, and think at the musical level of those who buy rock-and-roll records. He must subordinate his good taste and be heedless of the protestations of his inner self. He must think in musical terms that are so primitive that doltish children can respond. He must seek new and strange sounds, no matter how raucous or unmusical, sounds that will titillate tone-deaf teenagers. He needs inane songs that will gain acceptance in the mass market. He has to search for all kinds of devices (melodic, lyric, instrumental, rhythmic, or sound effect) that will cause millions of caterwauling kids to cut capers. He must take his job seriously, but, most of all, he must never take himself seriously.

Despite the vast difficulties of operating on an alien plane, the most successful rock-and-roll A. and R. men are musicians with extensive backgrounds in music of merit. Several, by staying alert, practicing one-upmanship, and fully understanding the least common denominator, have amassed fortunes.

The reader may be interested in learning to whom royalties, accruing from record sales, are distributed. Publishers and composers divide a share between them. Regardless of how many writers are responsible for one opus, they divide amongst themselves the same amount that would have gone to one composer had he been the sole author. The artist who is featured on the record and whose name appears in bold type receives royalty payments. If two or more artists work together, they divide the artist's share between them. If the recording is primarily instrumental, the orchestra leader whose name is featured or whose playing or conducting is featured receives the artist's royalties. Ordinarily, even if the album jacket features a singer's name and mentions (no matter how boldly) the name of the orchestra leader and, possibly, the names of the choir director and the arranger, only the artist receives the royalty payments. Sometimes when the conductor is of equal name value as the artist, an arrangement is worked out by which they both share in the royalties.

You may ask, "What about the musicians and background singers who are heard on the record? What about arrangers and orchestrators who so skillfully prepared the scores?" They receive nothing but their original fees.

Nevertheless, this huge industry is capable of putting a lot of money into a lot of people's pockets. It is a lucrative area for anyone who gets a big enough share of the work, and there are possibilities for anyone in recording. The player, arranger, or conductor who can come up with an idea that appeals to an A. and R. man (provided he can get close enough to an A. and R. man to explain and demonstrate his idea) will almost certainly be given an opportunity to convert his brain child into an album. One album that sells will surely lead to others. If you fail at first, you can always try again. Nothing is really lost and you will have gained a credit in the recording field.

Busy recording arrangers and conductors can enjoy long, well-paid careers in the recording field. The A. and R. man, working in a stratum that abounds in casualties, may make frequent switches from company to company or find some periods of not being able to secure a position, but if his ideas and judgment are sound, he will eventually find his place and enjoy an exceedingly profitable career.

CHAPTER VIII

Radio and Television

In the 1930s, radio was an important source of income for large numbers of musicians throughout the country. Network affiliates and independent stations almost universally carried regular complements of musicians on their staffs. Musicians associated with radio in the major music centers (New York, Chicago, and Los Angeles) were enjoying a heyday.

Sustaining (unsponsored) programs were usually played by staff orchestras, while commercially sponsored programs were played by free-lance musicians who were hired for specific shows. During those glorious days, it was not uncommon for free-lance musicians to earn seven or eight hundred dollars a week as they scurried from studio to studio, playing one program after another. Many of them were so busy that they were unable to appear at rehearsals and were permitted to send substitutes to mark accurately the parts to be played on the air. Consequently, these musicians often found themselves sight reading on the air, a position that, while lucrative to them, was not designed to result in optimum performance.

Later, the ground rules were changed to require the musician playing the show to take part in the entire rehearsal, and, in Los Angeles, in the interest of spreading the work among the growing number of musicians, a limit was placed on how many network programs free-lance musicians were allowed to play each week.

In New York, both NBC and Columbia put symphony orchestras to work on their staffs, and the practice of utilizing "house" musicians to play commercial programs grew as more and more air time was bought for commercial programming. Nevertheless, there was such an abundance of radio work available that free-lance musicians continued to thrive.

The situation remained a flourishing one until just after the end of World War II. About 1947, the general exodus of radio programs from New York to Hollywood, which had begun as a mere trickle several years earlier, became a veritable stampede. While New York musicians felt the pinch and had to depend more and more on recordings and transcriptions for a livelihood, Los Angeles became the factory for America's radio music. This left the New York network stations with large staff orchestras and not much work for them, but since commercial television, then in its infancy, gave promise of a bigger boom than ever, there was neither hysteria nor a mass migration to the west coast by New York musicians.

The television industry, ostensibly because it was young and not yet able to compete with radio, prevailed upon the American Federation of Musicians (the national union, as differentiated from the locals) to grant price concessions, and the Federation unwisely agreed. Because of this concession, the television stations, which had begun the practice of designing and packaging their own programs (formerly the prerogative of advertising agencies), discovered that it was often less expensive for them to employ free-lance musicians for television work, even if their own staffs were not operating on a full schedule. Thus, television opportunities grew by leaps and bounds while there was still some work, at least for staff men, in radio programs.

The radio-television industry, never one to be caught asleep, recognized the necessity for keeping staff men busy long before the musicians' union was fully aware of the situation and took steps to do something about it. Two acts of labor legislation, both of questionable merit, provided the springboards for action. On the one hand, a misguided court decision termed the union's requiring minimum numbers of musicians to be employed on the staffs of radio and television stations as "feather-bedding" and declared the practice unconstitutional. On the other hand, the union's belated attempt to prohibit the use by the network of recordings during certain prime broadcasting hours, while remaining silent about the unrestricted use of recordings in independent stations, resulted in a disastrous failure. These setbacks caused the abandonment of the Columbia Symphony and NBC's Symphony of the Air, and wholesale dismissals of staff musicians took place across the country. At the same time, disc jockeys and programs of recordings came into their own as the chief musical fare of the American radio public.

By the early 1950s, the television price scale was raised to become identical with radio scale. Live television shows employing musicians were fairly plentiful in New York, increasing in Los Angeles, and diminishing in Chicago. Local shows all over the rest of the country used their share of musicians, but the introduction of the coaxial cable, which made national hookups possible, dealt a death blow to the regular use of television orchestras on many local stations.

Because the hourly rate per man for free-lance musicians was much higher than the hourly rate for staff musicians and because of soaring television costs, the networks began to persuade advertisers to stop using free-lance orchestras, and, instead, to use orchestras composed of staff men. In the interest of economy, although we shall never know just how much saving was passed on to the sponsors, many advertisers consented to house orchestras provided personnel remained largely unchanged. Thus, in many instances whole orchestras, previously free-lance, were engaged as staff men. These men, of course, were not added to the staffs, but merely replaced other musicians who were let go. Sometimes, only a few of the free-lance men could be persuaded to join the staff. Some of those who refused were allowed to continue on the show as free-lance men. Others were replaced by house men. Naturally, these newly made staff musicians were given as full schedules as the stations could provide.

The result of all this was frequent turnovers in staff personnel, an urgent sense of insecurity among radio and television musicians, and a gradual obliteration of the concept of free-lance radio or television, at least in New York, as this former giant of TV suffered once again from the exodus of major live television programs to Hollywood, which had begun by the mid-Fifties.

But this new-found bonanza did not last long for Hollywood either. Most of the big musical variety shows had outlived their popularity. Dramatic shows became the important ones, and, while early dramatic shows were done live with original scores played live by musicians, the wealth of material on recordings, cleverly edited by music supervisors, soon proved an inexpensive method of replacing an otherwise modest music budget.

The use of the film-recorded show promised not only to exploit Hollywood film techniques, but to give Hollywood musicians ample opportunity for employment. This was not realized immediately, however, since film producers, seeking both tax relief and a method of utilizing the dollar credits that were piling up in European banks (as a result of leasing foreign rights to television films and kinescopes and because many European countries would not permit money to be taken out), began filming and recording in Europe. They soon discovered that because of the enormously lower European scales, music tracks made abroad offered quite a savings. Even many films made in this country had their music tracks recorded in Europe and shipped here. It is estimated that, at one time, over 65 percent of all American television music was recorded in Europe, while over 98 percent of our radio music is on recordings.

Today, an easing of restrictions against taking money out of foreign countries has combined with domestic pressure against foreign sound tracks for domestic use and the advent of advanced video-tape techniques to make Hollywood's filming and taping of television shows a booming business once again.

Still, the picture, as we see it today, is not a pretty one. Live music on local radio and television is reduced, for the most part, to an occasional hillbilly singer-guitarist, a gospel singer with piano or organ accompaniment, and very rarely any more than that. Several high-quality radio stations present a live chamber group or piano, piano-and-voice, or piano-and-violin recital at infrequent intervals, but this occurs so irregularly that the musician must consider it as nothing more than something extra. A few of our top symphonies have concerts regularly broadcast on radio, but this is rather an adjunct of the musician's income than an important separate source.

Studio work—that is radio, television, and recording jobs—has always demanded a very high level of musicianship from the players. The current surplus of highly qualified musicians over the jobs available has permitted an even greater degree of selectivity to be exercised than heretofore. The studio musician must be an accomplished instrumentalist, and his versatility must permit him to play convincingly any kind of music put before him. He must be equally at home whether he plays jazz, pop show, dance, or concert music. He must be adept at ensemble playing, and if called upon to play a solo passage, he must be able to play it with dispatch. His technical skill, his intonation, and his conception must at all times be impeccable. Besides, he must be a fluent sight reader and be well able to adapt himself to the idiosyncracies of various conductors.

Obviously, it takes years of training to prepare a musician for studio work—years of musical schooling and a wide background of varying musical experiences. The studio musician also has to be sympathetic to all kinds of music, or at least to understand all kinds of music so that he can give creditable and persuasive performances. These prerequisites are a challenge to any musician, so it is little wonder that a great many studio musicians are artists in their own right.

No specific education except music education is necessary for studio work. No résumés are required of prospective studio men. As in every other field, it is an advantage to be well liked, to stay out of other people's affairs, and to be tactful.

It is quite unusual for young, inexperienced conservatory graduates to enter the radio-television scene, although there are many conservatory graduates in the field. String players, French horn players, harpists, and other instrumentalists common to the symphony will generally have had a good concert background. This might include a symphony orchestra, ballet, opera orchestra, or perhaps some well-known chamber group. Other instrumentalists will have had dance-band experience, Broadway show experience, or a considerable back-ground in recordings.

Getting established in this field does not happen quickly. It means getting to know the contractors or conductors at the stations that employ musicians. A musician friend who works at the station can introduce the would-be studio man to his contractor and to his con-ductors. At this stage of the game, recommendations, reputation, and the quality of the musician's experience are important factors in determining whether or not he will be seriously considered. Name band experience is more important to a contractor than the *Prix de Rome*. Previous association with celebrities carries a good deal of weight, but in most cases it takes a good strong recommendation to cause a contractor to focus his attention on a newcomer and his record.

Since most station contractors occasionally contract musicians for a date not connected with the station, an opportunity to engage the television-bound musician may arise when one of these extracurricu-lar activities comes along. It might be a club date, a concert, or a recording, but when it does happen, you can be sure that the con-tractor, the conductor, and even the other musicians are observing and appraising his work carefully. If the novitiate comes through with flying colors, the contractor will place his name on a list where he can be kept in mind in the event a replacement is needed at the station.

No one can predict how long it will be from the first date until the musician is established in television. Many outside dates may be given him before he ever gets a chance to play at the station. Alto-gether, it is an exceedingly difficult field to gain entry to, and, I sup-pose, the man who gets in and succeeds in building a career should consider himself most fortunate, because it takes a good bit of luck to avoid being replaced in an industry that is characterized by change and upheaval.

By the early 1960's the staff musician began to phase out. A survey of 537 local radio and television stations in thirty-one states and the District of Columbia, but excluding New York, Chicago, and

Los Angeles, disclosed that 502 of these stations failed to employ a single live musician in 1960. The other thirty-five stations provided casual single engagements (generally less than four days' work in all of 1960) for 138 musicians, while an additional twenty-seven musicians were employed on a regular basis.

Only a few of the outlets of the major radio-television networks (CBS, NBC and ABC) retained musicians on their staffs. The outlets at New York and Los Angeles were the last bastions to fall. At CBS in New York, only fifty of the sixty-five staff musicians were being kept busy and by the mid-1960's the final phasing out began in earnest. As of January 31, 1974, CBS took the last musician off its payroll and they, like the other networks, offer musicians work through what is termed "casual employment"—that is, on a date by date basis.

CBS currently spends approximately four million dollars annually in New York and the West Coast on this casual employment. The average musician earns $300 per show for a one hour variety show. This includes pay for four hours of rehearsal (which he receives even if he rehearses for only one-half hour) and one hour of actual performance. For a "strip" show of the Johnny Carson or Mike Douglas type, which includes virtually no rehearsal, he gets $1000 for a five day week with a two hour show each day.

The station's contractor hires musicians at the suggestion of the conductor or whoever is in charge of the music for that particular show. Technically, the contractor is the musician's representative, the liaison between employees and management. His duties are, strictly speaking, administrative. He is responsible for personnel. He alone hires or dismisses, although these functions are usually performed at someone else's behest. He is responsible for apportioning the work among the musicians, for drawing up the weekly schedules, and for seeing that there are neither overlapping nor conflicting rehearsals or shows for his men. It is his responsibility to see to it that musicians appear on time for engagements and that discipline is maintained. His loyalty to the company obliges him to avoid overtime payments to musicians wherever possible, and, at all other times, to juggle their schedules so deftly that unavoidable overtime payments are kept at a minimum. Finally, he is responsible for all billing for musicians' work.

Since the contractor is frequently on the move, going from one date to another, and rarely in one place for any length of time, and because of the manifold nature of his duties, he is usually given an office and a staff of one or more assistants. Although his assistants share his work load for him, the final responsibility for every decision or action originating in his office is his alone; thus, the position of station contractor becomes essentially a one-man operation.

The contractor is well paid for his services. In New York, his salary must be at least double the minimum rate prevailing at his station. In addition, the contractor's reputation for efficiency and his numerous dealings with free-lance conductors puts him in a position to contract many outside free-lance dates (single engagements not connected with his work as staff contractor). At least one man, to my knowledge, by combining his income from being a station's contractor with that earned from contracting regularly a large number of outside engagements, has become a wealthy man.

The station contractor's position is usually offered to a man because of his reputation as a contractor or because of some strong personal tie between a contractor and one or more company executives who either are empowered to offer the position or can exert enough pressure to have their choice selected. No amount of musical study will prepare a man for such a job, but practical experience as a musician is an indispensable training ground for acquiring the potential contractor with the essential facts of the contractor's life. Although men filling such positions enjoy long, profitable careers, the very real scarcity of opportunity in this department renders pointless the preparation by the young musician for such a career. Only the circumstances of his life and the situations with which he becomes involved can determine whether or not he will ever have a chance of becoming a staff contractor.

The free-lance radio-television musician can supplement his income by teaching. Devoting several hours a week to teaching will not only provide additional income but can prove a worthy crutch to lean upon in times of stress.

All things considered, the musician's lot as a free-lance radio-television performer is a mixed blessing. Once established, the renumeration for such work is in the top stratum. But, of course, he has no assurance of steady employment and the time and amount of his working hours can be erratic.

Although the nature of the music generally played by radio-television orchestras in this country rarely demands more than competent craftsmanship, the quality of musicians thus employed is usually so high that it is a delight to sit in such orchestras and take part in the musical experience.

CHAPTER IX

A Touch of Jazz

The jazz artist is a breed of musician who possesses many of the qualities of the concert artist. He may not undergo the same strict regimen of training, but his sensitivity is great and his musicianship is developed to an extraordinary level. He is wonderfully facile at imitation and he has remarkable talents for invention. He combines artistic integrity with vivid imagination. He has no qualms about pushing forward the frontiers of jazz style, nor about reaching back into the past for an appropriate idea. He has what too many other musicians lack: ears that really hear. In short, like the concert artist, he is an outstanding member of his field.

Naturally, not all jazz musicians are artists. Many are excellent copies of more perfect models. Most follow the patterns established by the artists, and lack the imagination to be really creative. Hundreds upon hundreds of jazz exponents learn to improvise convincingly and are versatile, thoroughly skilled players. Theirs is a valid artistic expression.

Back in the 1930s, after the jazz musician had finished his apprenticeship in the gin mills and hot spots, he had numerous opportunities to join big bands and play with many of the jazz players in the country. Out of that period came Benny Goodman, Artie Shaw, Duke Ellington, and Count Basie. Conditions for jazz expression continued to be good until after World War II. As if endowed with foreknowledge, little bands and combos began springing up everywhere during the war—years before there was an indication of the decline of big bands.

Big bands continued to get bigger until no hotels or dance halls could support them. An occasional jazz concert was all that was left of the big band jazz era.

Meanwhile, the little bands began to gain recognition, for the new styles in which they played were ideally suited to the instrumentations they used. Names began to emerge and the combos became big attractions.

When, finally, rock and roll swept the country, the youngsters who were so taken by it began to resist jazz stubbornly. This had the effect of cutting tremendously into those clubs that·once had employed non-name and semi-name jazz groups.

There were but few places like Birdland where jazz connoisseurs could gather to hear their favorite name combos and this kind of limited booking kept the name groups fairly well occupied. However, the former jazz spots began to book bizarre entertainer-musicians, the kind who wear funny hats and make strange noises. The result was that, except for a small number of so-called joints, the budding jazz musician no longer had a training ground to develop his talents and the veteran had no place to keep his talents sharp and his lips wet.

Gerry Mulligan, whose quartet became internationally famous and whose talents are awesome, decided to form a "large" ten-piece band. He wrote wonderful, inspired things for this group and reaction to it was all that could be desired. However, economic problems made it impossible to book the band for more than a few weeks each year.

One would think that economic adversity or personal misfortunes would tend to stifle the creative efforts of jazz musicians. However, this is not the case. Jazz and jazz musicians have remarkable vitality, and in the face of the worst kinds of reverses they stand up and play with a freshness and vigor that gives no hint of woe or cares.

In the 1960's the pendulum started a swing back in the other direction. More and more jazz activity sprang up in clubs and concerts and festivals. Jazz education began to grow and gain a more confident voice in the hallowed halls of higher education. Jazz clinics were initiated in several areas. Here veteran jazz men were engaged to teach and coach talented youngsters who otherwise might have had no opportunity to gain big jazz band experience. The student arrangers got to hear their products professionally played by the faculty members.

Also in the 1960's, rock began to make inroads into jazz, and there was a consequent turning to the basic rock resource of electrification. By the 1970's many artists had converted to a jazz-rock style though some stick to a straight jazz format. Foremost among the former is pianist-composer Herbie Hancock whose group features electronic keyboards and synthesizers.

Jazz had a real revival around 1973 and now maintains a secure niche in the eclectic musical world of the 70's. Its popularity was proved at the ten day 1974 Newport Jazz Festival in New York City which drew 200,000 people. Monterey, California hosted another successful jazz festival that year.

The 1970's also saw the opening of new jazz clubs in New York City's Greenwich Village and the upper West Side. The Roseland Ballroom held a thirties ball featuring the bands of Woody Herman, Duke Ellington and Count Basie.

In May of 1974 the jazz world sustained a great loss with the death of composer-bandleader Duke Ellington. But the Duke lives on in the Duke Ellington Orchestra which continues to perform here and abroad.

CHAPTER X

Hotel, Cafe, and Night Club

Tinkling rhythms and rock, show tunes and floor shows, society orchestras and combos, are part and parcel of night spots to be found all over the country—in fact, all over the world. From honky-tonks to smart supper clubs one finds an assortment of musical offerings that vary from fifteen- or twenty-piece orchestras down to boy-and-girl duos and solo pianists. Thousands of places present a bewildering variety of music. An evening of dancing or a night of listening to jazz are as easy to find in our urban centers as the entertainment page in the local newspaper. The velvet quiet of strings to provide the backdrop to elegant dining, a strolling trio to play requests as they pass the table where you enjoy a cocktail, the pianist who sings in the hotel lounge typify the topsy-turvy world of the night club musician who sleeps while the rest of the world is rising and who works while the rest of the world plays or sleeps. The dance hall, the beer garden, the cabaret, the restaurant, the hotel dining room, the night club, the tavern, the inn, or even the ocean liner are all his milieu.

More musicians are employed, deployed, and then unemployed in this area than in any other field of musical activity. In no other area does there exist a greater disparity in the talents and musical skills of those working in this category, nor is any other field so lacking in the standardization of the qualities necessary to play specific engagements satisfactorily. In no other area is the rate of pay so low or the insecurity so high. Yet there are those in this field whose lives are spent, more or less regularly employed, happily playing the kinds of music demanded, successfully accommodating their living expenses to their potential incomes, and who are not only unresentful of being so low on the totem pole but are downright thankful for their skills and their jobs.

Some groups play a wide variety of music. Others are limited to one or two types. Some play Latin music exclusively; others only light concert music and operettas. Some specialize in jazz; some play only floor shows and an occasional dance set. Society orchestras play only the melodies of the best-known tunes, replete with florid piano embellishments, at brisk tempos, and are usually enjoined from playing jazz. Gypsy music and so-called ethnic music are played against appropriate settings. In some orchestras the emphasis is on style and musical ability, while in others the pendulum comes full swing, and the music is of secondary importance, with the emphasis being on the entertainment qualities of the players.

Some groups play almost entirely from memory, thus rendering totally unnecessary the ability of their musicians to sight read fluently. Those groups that have their arrangements written out require varying degrees of sight-reading ability, although usually a limited skill is sufficient. On the other hand, places with extravagant floor shows demand excellent sight readers with highly developed instrumental skills and versatility. Some establishments employ unbelievably poor musicians, and others are fortunate to secure the services of truly superb musicians.

Most musicians in this field are paid the minimum scale, but small combinations (generally of three to eight people) that have achieved a name are able to find more employment opportunities at prices considerably above minimum scale than their less fortunate, comparatively anonymous brother musicians. The name groups, however, are usually found to have considerable entertainment value; their most lucrative bookings are in the lounges of Las Vegas.

In 1974, superstars like Elvis Presley and Frank Sinatra (both of whom made comebacks) were earning $250,000 a week at a Las Vegas hotel. Diana Ross and Ann-Margret command weekly salaries of $150,000, and a popular vocal group like Gladys Knight and the Pips get extraordinary pay, also.

The policies of the owners and managers of the establishments that employ orchestras vary considerably. A few hire leaders to supply orchestras and are content never to make a change. Consequently, some leaders have remained at the same hotel or restaurant (usually hotel) for up to twenty or more years. A similar attitude on the part of some of these "resident" leaders has enabled some musicians to remain on the same jobs with them for many, many years. Normally, however, managers of dining rooms and clubs think a change of faces is good for business. How often they change is a matter of personal preference. Some keep an orchestra for a few years, but others change every few months, and still others insist on a new orchestra every two weeks. (One entrepreneur in suburban New York City considers himself both enlightened and benevolent since he regularly employs a quartet and always keeps a group six weeks before bringing in a new one.)

The transitory nature of this kind of employment creates serious problems for large numbers of helpless musicians. Having done a competent (and appreciated) job, these men find themselves dismissed through no fault of their own, and because of circumstances utterly beyond their control. The great problem confronting such men is that there are a great many more available orchestras than jobs. Therefore, protracted periods of being "between engagements" seriously hamper many a musician's ability to support himself.

A statistical evaluation of this situation would require a battery of electronic computers, because even if the number of steady and single engagements taken part in each day—say, in New York— were known, the situation changes so rapidly from day to day that an army of mathematicians would be unable to reduce the number of jobs done to the number of people performing them; to determine how many of the thirty thousand New York musicians depend wholly or partially on music or are independent of it; or to determine which musicians dismissed from steady jobs are performing single engagements; and thus to arrive at significant figures to evaluate the amount and effect of unemployment arising in this area. Suffice it to say that this writer is well acquainted with any number of competent players who are habitually confronted with longer periods of unemployment than of employment.

Some fortunate groups operating in this field have been successful in booking a yearly circuit for themselves so that they more or less regularly play at several different locations, and return periodically to the starting point to begin the circuit anew. Others alternate between a hotel or resort establishment in the south during the winter season and play in a similar establishment in the north during the summer. All told, such alternations may produce as much as eight to ten months' work annually.

The best opportunities rest with leaders who, failing to become name leaders, develop into what is known as semi-names and who become fixtures in one job or in a certain class of jobs. (The semi-name is a name of relative importance at the local or regional level, while names are national and international in repute.) All leaders receive extra money for being leaders. Thus, semi-name leaders who work with fair regularity in positions where higher scales prevail are likely to pursue fairly remunerative careers, which may possibly be long-lived. However, since such leaders have direct contact with their public, the degree of their success usually reflects their personal qualities; affability, magnetism, and the like are persuasive factors.

The same qualities of personality are requisite in the successful solo pianist whose wage scale is generally at least 25 percent higher than the minimum scale. Not only getting along well with his public but possessing those qualities that produce groups of admirers and entice them back time after time are the hallmarks of success in pursuing the solo pianist's profession. The kinds of music he will play are generally dictated by the manager of the room, the clientele, and his own taste. He may be a brilliant pianist or he may be thoroughly unskilled. (I have heard a number of remarkably incompetent solo pianists who were literally adored by their audiences. Personable qualities plus confidence plus a rudimentary familiarity with some portions of all the melodies requested endeared them to the hearts of their listeners. It mattered not a whit to the adorers that a total ignorance of the harmonic patterns turned otherwise nauseating performances into sheer impossibilities.) Nevertheless, even the most compelling solo pianist's success will be an image of his personal effect on his listeners.

New York, Chicago, and Los Angeles have more of this work to offer than most other cities, although there are many orchestras employed in such cities as San Francisco, New Orleans, Kansas City, Boston, Minneapolis, Cleveland, Miami (and Miami Beach), to mention a few. Most cities have at least one hotel orchestra and a few cafe or dance hall combos, besides cocktail lounge groups. Las Vegas is a veritable oasis for musicians. However, in recent travels I discovered at least a few cities in which not one single musician was steadily employed.

Throughout most of the country, the work week is six nights. Chicago gives its musicians two nights off each week, and Las Vegas, where relief bands used to come in one night each to relieve the regular on its night off, is reported to maintain a seven-night work week at the present time.

Union scales vary from locality to locality. The number of hours worked is also significant in determining the weekly wage as is also the union's classification of the place of business. The scales in Las Vegas are reputedly the highest in the country; those of New York are traditionally high as are Chicago's. The scales in the rest of the country range from less to least.

A side man in a Class "A" hotel, restaurant, or night club in Manhattan earns $304.04. This is on the basis of six nights per week (five nights for $258.38 plus $50.66 for a "night off"), five-six hours work per night. Because of the sophistication of the audiences who frequent such places, a high degree of musical skills and competency is essential to each employment. The leader earns from $380.05 to $607 depending on the number of men in the group. Overtime runs $15.17 an hour and rehearsals are $12 an hour for a minimum of two hours plus $6.00 for any added hours or part of an hour. Doubling on an instrument brings an additional $2.00 per day and another $1.00 a day for a second doubling.

Obviously, this is not a lucrative field for the musician. Wages are frequently low, unemployment is high, and, to compound the musician's difficulties, phonograph records and piped-in music have waged a remorseless war against his employment opportunities.

Still, it cannot be denied that a small percentage of those engaged in the field have found some measure of satisfaction there. Some non-names plod away year after year, just make a living, and manage to exist. A few semi-names, especially leaders in better paying jobs, can be considered quite successful by most standards. They earn livings above $20,000, lead full, rewarding lives, and are respected and civic-minded citizens in their communities. Name band musicians earn the most of any side men in this area, being paid quite well, while the leaders of such bands have remarkable earning power because of a remarkable drawing power. Name bands do much to stir up interest in live music and are thus an aid to the less well-paid, less well-known musicians who are striving in the same field.

CHAPTER XI

Man with a Stick

The man known as the leader, who may or may not conduct, is in effect the head of a business enterprise. This enterprise, whether or not it has artistic aims, certainly has an objective—to make money for the leader.

Many leaders are highly competent musicians. Successful leaders of big-band days were people of initiative, perseverance, and business acuity. The most successful of them appeared to have some sort of personal magnetism or glamor that gave their music another dimension, at least in the eyes of their admirers.

Today, in much of our studio work there are many successful leaders who never have any personal contact with the public. These men are more like musicians than business men; more like conductors than leaders; and, frequently, more like arrangers than anything else.

Anyone can be a leader who can talk some club owner into letting him book a band there. Many careers have begun in just that fashion, but the name band leaders were usually musicians of repute who were successful in getting large financial backing to help launch their ventures, and many more failed than succeeded.

Today, one might get started by organizing and rehearsing a small band for a couple of months. It would have to be small because, according to Woody Herman and others, present-day economics do not permit the huge payrolls that large bands entail. When the band's repertoire has become sufficiently varied and extensive and the play-

ing smooth enough, the leader either arranges live auditions for booking agents or he sets out to record demonstration tapes. This latter
is even a better idea because by pressing demonstration records from
the tapes he can not only take them around to agents but can possibly, by playing his records for recording company executives, be
lucky enough to be offered a recording contract. If any booking
agent should take a fancy to the group's sound, and if he should
foresee a chance of promoting the group, he might hasten to sign
the leader and his combo, get on the 'phone to try to place the group
in a spot, and, if successful, a new career might well be on its way.

In the field of free-lance studio work, musicians from the ranks
from time to time happen into situations whereby an opportunity to
become a leader is offered them. Sometimes a musician who enjoys
a particularly close relationship with a show-business personality
gets the opportunity to become his conductor. He may have worked
on a TV show with this star, or the kinship may have had its incep-
tion in recording sessions. Perhaps the musician already has been the
arranger, accompanist, or conductor for the personality on a road
tour and so, should this singer or comedian (or whatever he may be)
get his own TV show, the chance to elevate his musician friend to
the rank of leader arises.

Although a variety of hypothetical cases (the above is actual)
might be cited to show how men become leaders, the truth is that
circumstances seem to play a much larger role than determination in
effecting the change from player to conductor, and the number of
such opportunities is not unduly large. Nevertheless, such strokes of
fate do occur and new conductors come into being. What happens
from this point forward in the career of a new leader is not always
strictly under his control, but the man with charm and tact whose
work measures up to the faith put in him will usually experience a
steady growth in stature and work opportunities, and his income can
be expected to keep pace with this growth.

There are inherent dangers in making the jump from player to
leader. Occasionally, the new leader may not have had sufficient
conducting experience to tackle a difficult, exacting job. An inability
to remember correct tempos, especially in a fast-moving show, may

bring complaints from people whose performances may, as a result, be spoiled. A complicated ballet or operatic score, placed with little warning on the inexperienced conductor's show, may bewilder him to the point of panic. Worst of all, speeding up tempos or stretching slow songs may cause a show to be a couple of minutes short or to run over, in which case the new conductor may be fair game for the sponsor.

Further, a year or two of being a leader or a conductor does not guarantee future work in this area. Many conductors do not like to hire men who are or have been conductors, since they appear to pose some kind of threat to their jobs, so the conductor without too many credits who finds himself suddenly without any conducting assignments, may experience a difficult time getting jobs playing his instrument again.

On the other hand, if things go fairly smoothly, as they frequently do, an income varying from good to magnificent may ensue. The established conductor in one area may go on to positions of dominance in several other areas, and if he should happen to go into the moving picture field and excel, he will make an enormous salary.

When we come to the subject of conducting, as it refers to the symphony orchestra or other art music, we are dealing with an area in which the conductor is far more than a time-beater. The conductor, in this context, is truly an artist on a level with the finest concert artists. His instrument is the orchestra, which he controls by means of hand gestures, bodily movements, and facial expressions. His training is much the same as the concert artist's, except that not only does he have to become a virtuoso in conducting techniques, but he should be a skilled player of one or more instruments, and, according to Herman Scherchen in his "Handbook of Conducting," be able to play *all* the instruments of the orchestra, at least rudimentarily.

In addition to having a knowledge of musical literature and the history of music that is all embracing, his liberal education and his reading should be extensive. Little disconcerts the educated symphony musician more than to play under a conductor whose manners are boorish, whose speech is vulgar, and whose education is inferior.

Moreover, there is such a great kinship between music and literature (especially poetry) that many conductors have traditionally derived much inspiration for their performances from exploring the profundities in books.

The conductor must be a man of confident bearing, a man who commands attention and whose gestures have the stamp of authority. His stock-in-trade is his distinctness and clarity with the baton. In like manner, his command of language should be impeccable, so that, in the least possible time and in the most direct manner, he can find the exact words to explain precisely what is needed of his players, what he desires of them. The articulate conductor, by the intelligent choice of words that clearly point up the most delicate shades of his intent, can save himself a thousand futile gestures. (Toscanini, who never became fluent in English, was wont, in fits of frustration, to scream epithets in Italian at his errant players.) It is the conductor's great musical mastery and his ability to give expression to it, both by gesture and by word, that cause the modern orchestra to appear as one of the artistic miracles of our time.

The young conductor is advised to conduct wherever he can— amateur concerts, summer festivals, and college and conservatory orchestras—and he is urged to continue his studies. Unfortunately, there are not enough orchestras with regular seasons to provide conducting posts for all the fine young talent that exists. However, a position with a secondary orchestra provides experience and notices, even if no sustained income is possible. Study, if you can, with a name conductor. Should he decide to take you under his wing, good things could happen. If you are an apt student and he is impressed with your progress, perhaps an assistant conductorship may be in the offing. Given a few lucky breaks and a warm press, you could be but a few steps from your own orchestra, or some other post of honor and reward. Perhaps a road company opera tour may lead to La Scala and thence to the Metropolitan Opera. Perhaps Hollywood awaits you!

Today, the conductor, with his autocratic powers over the orchestra, is a dominating figure. Upon him the musical attention of the masses is focused. He, the personification of virtuosity, is lionized by multitudes of worshippers. His interpretations are considered to be the last word. His gesticulations and eccentricities are looked upon as solemn ceremonial rites. More attention is paid to his antics than to his music.

This could happen to you, and you would make tremendous amounts of money. Of course, you could never hope to make as much money as, say, Jack Benny did in his lifetime. But, then, who really needs that much money?

CHAPTER XII

Arrangers, Orchestrators, and Copyists

At least 90 percent of all music that is performed by musicians has first been arranged or orchestrated and then extracted from score onto individual parts by copyists. Most arrangers, orchestrators, and copyists are employed on a free-lance basis and paid for piece-work. That is, arrangers and orchestrators receive so much for each four-measure page of scoring, the rate depending upon the number of staves employed and the medium for which the score is intended. Copyists are paid either an hourly rate or, more frequently, a rate based on the nature of the work for each page produced.

Successful arrangers and orchestrators must be thoroughly familiar with the idioms of each of the instruments for which they write. They must also be extremely facile in handling complex tonal textures. In other words, they must know the relative tonal weights of different instrumental colors when used in combination or played off one against the other, and they must know how these tonal weights vary according to register. The skillful orchestrator knows which color will predominate when colors are mixed, and he knows which doublings may be necessary to make individual melodic or contrapuntal lines stand out, although, in the case of music written for a recorded or broadcast medium, the judicious placement of microphones can lend a helping hand.

The arranger performs all the duties of the orchestrator and, in addition, is responsible for reharmonization, paraphrasing, or development of a composition already complete in form. He invents introductions, modulations, endings, and counter-melodies, as well as ostinato-type figures and fragmentary fills.

Orchestrators, whose sketch may include all the details of a complete composition, are usually not permitted such latitude in matters of invention. With all of the details of melody, counter-melody, harmony, rhythm, and figuration supplied to him, it is the orchestrator's responsibility to transform such a sketch into an orchestral score. The choice of colors, the determination of which parts to harmonize and which to leave bare, and the option of doubling and change of register are his.

Busy commercial arrangers and orchestrators rarely have time for experimentation. Consequently, they draw upon their experience to furnish them with innumerable orchestral devices that have been previously tested and proven. It is left for the experimental, non-commercial arranger or orchestrator to invent and try out new devices. Such men are frequently composers who need not be committed to firm deadlines and whose imaginations can be given free rein as they take their time and labor as patiently and lovingly over each successive phase as a mother over her new-born babe. It has been said that to be a successful arranger-orchestrator, all one needs is to have a keen memory for all the best orchestral devices one has ever heard plus the ability to re-create remembered colors and patterns.

Although considerable study plus a familiarity with the orchestral techniques of the masters is recommended, nothing takes the place of hearing, in person, orchestrations one has written. By hearing one's work and by comparing the desired effect with that which actually resulted, one establishes numerous points of reference for improvement and refinement.

The orchestrators and arrangers whose talents are most used find that they have numerous deadlines to meet each week. Consequently, they have learned that speed together with accuracy are indispensable. The fastest of these may score from four to eight or more pages an hour, depending upon the nature of the material. Numerous short-cuts have been adopted as the common practice of arrangers and orchestrators and their copyists are relied upon to understand and observe what is meant. For example, when parts are in unison, the word "col" followed by the name of the instrument to which it has reference will alert the copyist to extract the correct part. Suppose that four trombones are to be written in unison. Trombone I has his part completely written out, but each of the other trombone parts will have the notation "col Trombone I." Even if the part to be copied is not written at the proper octave or needs to be transposed, say, from trumpet II to 'cello, the first note is written to indicate register and transposition and the rest of the phrase is indicated by "col Trumpet II."

The use of "come sopras" is another device that is a short-cut for arrangers. When an arranger finds that a number of measures in one section are identical with those of a previous section (of the same arrangement), he merely indicates "come sopra," designates the letter or page number to be copied, and the measure; for example, if the first four measures of (C) are identical to the first four measures of (A), the first measure of (C) would bear the legend "come sopra (A1)" and the next three would be marked (A2), (A3), and (A4).

Some arrangers have copyists who are fine arrangers themselves and frequently can be entrusted with filling in large sections of scores. Thus, when the opportunity presents itself and time is pressing heavily on the arranger, he may completely fill out all the parts for the first note of a given section, to indicate his choice of voicing (open, close, or the manner of his preference) and then, by indicating the succeeding harmonies, leave the filling in of the unwritten parts to the copyist.

The income earned by arrangers and orchestrators is, of course, in direct proportion to the amount and type of work they are assigned to score. The busiest of them are subject to frequent all-night sessions, but the rewards are extremely good. Our most active arrangers and orchestrators earn up to $75,000 a year, or more. However, most busy arrangers are in the $20,000–$30,000 bracket, while there are many competent arrangers whose incomes remain fairly fixed in the $12,000–$15,000 range.

Scoring for motion pictures, TV, phonograph records, and Broadway musicals are among the best-paying arrangers' and orchestrators' opportunities. Night club, dance band, and similar work pays less, although many arrangers earn splendid livings scoring exclusively for singers, comics, and others who need arrangements for their night-club acts. Besides, nothing prevents an arranger from charging above the minimum union scale if he can get it.

The young musician who desires to become an arranger or orchestrator is advised to score for anything and everything that comes his way. By so doing, he will be improving his technique while he is building his reputation. The more of this he does the better, since an expanding circle of personal contacts will eventually give him the opportunity to gain a real foothold in the field, provided his skills are competitive. Phonograph records provide easily accessible models with which to compare one's work as well as a source to rejuvenate flagging inspiration.

Copyists, who work hand-in-hand with arrangers and orchestrators, are an indispensable part of the music-supplying field. Their ability to decipher illegible scores and to understand all the short-cuts arrangers use is a tribute to their patience and ingenuity, and frequently, since many correct the errors inadvertently made in the score, to their musicianship.

They are often called upon to work around the clock, to pick up scores, and deliver finished parts. Their work is expected to be neat, accurate, and extremely legible; above all, they are expected to be fast. In addition, they are also frequently called upon for transposing, editing, and proofreading. Nevertheless, their financial return is considerably less than that of the arrangers whose work they get out.

Their complete dependence upon arrangers necessitates their working in those cities and areas where arrangers and orchestrators enjoy the most employment. New York, Chicago, Los Angeles, and Las Vegas are the biggest centers for both arranger-orchestrators and copyists. Copying can provide a very satisfactory income for the busy copyists, some of whom regularly earn in excess of $20,000 per year. Chief copyists and supervisors with Broadway shows, films and TV can earn more.

Some copyists have opened offices that specialize in copying services. They employ a staff of copyists, invest in equipment such as drafting tables, pianos, special lights, copying supplies, and duplicating machines. While it is true that such men do not become captains of industry, they do manage, if they acquire enough regular accounts, to manage flourishing little businesses. One such service regularly copies Menotti's operas. Another does all the copying for one busy Broadway musical producer. Some regularly prepare all the manuscripts for a weekly musical TV show.

Gaining entry into the copying field is a matter of personal contact. Helping a copyist when he is overloaded with work, or being recommended by a friend who is a copyist can turn the trick. Above all, the requisite skills must reside in the individual desiring to pursue copying as a career.

CHAPTER XIII

The Serious Composer

If the concert artist and the conductor are the masters of musical analysis, the composer is the master of synthesis. Whether he composes guided by instinct and inspiration alone or after many years of diligent study of the various materials used in composition, in no way alters the fact that he is putting together elements of melody, harmony, rhythm, counterpoint, and orchestration. However, it is not the skill with which he puts these elements together that determines the quality of his compositions. Almost anyone, through assiduous imitation of existing models, can become deft in the handling of the different elements of composition. The composer demonstrates his talent through his invention and originality, by his taste and inspiration. These are portrayed by the manner in whch he causes musical ideas to grow dynamically.

His ability to develop a melodic fragment, to build and join musical phrases and sentences, to sense when to modulate, to know how to modulate effectively, to balance large sections of major compositions architecturally—these are certainly skills that can be developed. But the source of the skills is within the individual and is a reflection of his inspiration and imagination. These skills do not devolve from proficiency in harmony, counterpoint, and orchestration, which are merely the tools that, when well learned, may be used more or less automatically to express the musical ideas that develop in the composer's mind. The better the knowledge of these theoretical subjects, the more facile is the technique of composition, but it does not follow that the quality of composition is superior; that intrinsic quality of a composition is a function of the composer's inner resources.

As an analogy let me cite the operations in taking a motor trip. Before one can drive an automobile, one must learn the techniques of starting the engine, shifting the gears, operating the accelerator and the brake pedal, and guiding the vehicle by means of the steering wheel. Once these basic skills are learned, the operator is ready for his trip. However, the mechanical skills are performed almost automatically, and although their presence is felt and necessity for having and using these skills is obvious, the important thing about the trip is the start, the direction toward a destination, and the safe arrival at the destination. The quality of the trip depends upon the smoothness of the ride, the contours of the roads, the scenery, and the successful conclusion to the ride. The mechanical skills are necessary, of course, but the real adventure is the manner and route of travel and the destination.

Thus, our best composers are exceptionally facile in handling the materials of their medium and they enjoy creative gifts that enable them to invent works of originality, works whose emotional and intellectual content is so powerful that they equal or surpass the greatest of art expression in any other field. Our best composers are caught up in a frenzy of musical outpourings, and set aside certain hours each day for composition.

Is there a future for such ardent creators? Artistically, yes. Financially, no!

No art composer can possibly support himself from earnings derived from his compositions unless, like Georges Auric, he is able to compose a movie score as often as he needs. The sad truth is that there is no market for new art compositions. The occasional grant or commission of a new work rarely brings a sufficiently large stipend to sustain a composer and his family. Even the many competitions for younger composers bring only nominal monetary rewards. All serious art composers who lack large personal fortunes find that necessity dictates their pursuing other careers for their subsistence.

William Schuman, prominent American composer and former

president of the Juilliard School of Music in New York City, wrote, "There is probably no composer today who can earn as much money from publication of music as he can by writing textbooks or articles about music. It seems to me that the educationalists are missing an enormous opportunity by not asking contemporary composers to write for their schools. It would cost them no more than the regular purchase price of music because thousands of copies would be involved and the large guaranteed sale could serve in lieu of the more conventional commission."

This points dramatically to the economic peril that faces the art composer. Juilliard's current president, Peter Mennin, pursues a career in education and administration. Our colleges and music schools are full of composers who have become teachers in order to exist. This limits the amount of time that they can devote to composition, but does not prohibit it. Further, it explains the frenzy that dominates the composer's after-school hours.

Careers in music education, while compromises, at best are the most practical compromises, since they keep composers steeped in music, in a stimulating intellectual atmosphere, and give him the kind of security he needs. Much could be written attacking conditions that make it necessary for composers to lead dual lives, but its value lies in the fact that such an arrangement makes it possible for music students to study at firsthand and work closely with these men. Such relationships can only profit the ambitious and talented student.

Furthermore, the composer-teacher of authority is able to derive considerable additional income from the writing of textbooks and articles, just as William Schuman wrote.

It must be remarked that despite the adverse economic conditions under which our art composers must work, original composition in America is flourishing, and some of the brightest talents in the world are numbered among our American composers.

CHAPTER XIV

The Commercial Composer

The field of commercial composition breaks down into two separate, but in some instances mutually overlapping, areas. The first is that of the serious commercial composer, and the other that of the song writer.

The serious commercial composer may, in fact, be a serious art composer who is also enjoying the fruits of commercial composition. He may have all the talent and skill of the art composer, yet have no particular drive to create art music, and so is content to turn his talents to something more rewarding materially. Certainly, the best commercial composers have much of the training and have developed many of the skills of their counterparts in the art field. Their work is chiefly concerned with writing for pictures and for TV. Others have entered the TV-commercial field by writing background music for short commercial films. Since all of this area is covered in detail elsewhere in this volume, let us go on to an examination of the field of song writing.

The song writer (not to be confused with the composer of art songs who is a serious art composer) may also have all the skills and talents of our masters. More often, however, his musical training is far less extensive. All he really needs is a talent for creating melodies that are vocal in nature and not too difficult to remember. Some of our most untutored talents have made fortunes writing songs. Irving Berlin was famous for his transposing piano, which permitted him to play everything in the key of C. Bob Merrill, composer of the one-time Broadway hit, *Carnival,* was said to compose all his tunes on a toy xylophone.

Today, the business of song writing is extraordinarily rewarding and extremely difficult to enter. The dominance of the recording industry over the publishing industry coupled with the importance of rock and roll have all but obliterated Tin Pan Alley. It is no longer possible to approach the music publishers armed with a briefcase full of songs, with the same hope for success that prevailed, say, thirty years ago. It is true that some songs are still placed in that fashion, but in the real Tin Pan Alley days if a publisher liked a song, he published it. Sales of sheet music and orchestrations brought royalties whether it was recorded or not. Recordings only added to the income from songs.

Today, however, only those publishers who enjoy access to A. and R. men or recording artists will take songs. If they feel strongly about a song's potentiality, publishers will spend money to prepare a demonstration record of it to submit to a recording company or to an artist. The artist can usually only suggest to the A. and R. man, who usually has the final OK. If such songs are recorded, they get published. If they are not accepted by an A. and R. man and recorded, they do not get published. Only a few song writers are able to get songs published in this manner, and most of them are old-timers, well known by the publishers and with many credits in Tin Pan Alley.

Jerry Adler, who wrote the music to at least two Broadway hit musicals tried his hand with the publishers and A. and R. men and got exactly nowhere. In desperation, he turned to the jingle field, and his Newport cigarette jingle was a standout. Jerry, in a TV interview, observed that the competition caused by innumerable rock-and-roll writers, the most successful of whom rise to the fore with one or two hit records and then drop back to obscurity, had ruined the song writing business.

However, the potential song writer, if he is disposed to write in the popular idiom of the day (rock and roll, western, and the like), is urged to try the field. More than a few such writers, although it must be confessed that most of them are also recording artists, have consistently recorded hits they themselves have written.

A perfect springboard for the song writer is a close relationship with a recording artist who has the power to select his own material. The writer can enjoy the unique experience of being commissioned to write specifically for the artist. Such a position was enjoyed by the team of Jimmy Van Heusen and Sammy Cahn who wrote many title songs for Frank Sinatra albums. A combination of talents like these are not likely to go unnoticed, nor are they likely to fail to produce wide sales. A string of successes could easily lead to motion pictures or the Broadway theatre. (In the case of Van Heusen and Cahn, they wrote for the movies *before* they wrote for Sinatra.)

Movie producers are not apt to ignore writers with a knack for turning out successful songs. An offer to write a title theme or to compose a number of songs for a movie is not one to be taken lightly. In fact, it is the goal toward which many talented song writers strive, the goal that few ever attain. The ability to have turned out a number of successful songs is one of the prime requisites of song writing for the movies, but since it is now so much more difficult than heretofore for the legitimate song writer (as opposed to the rock and roller) to get songs recorded and thus have produced hits, the changes of preparing the groundwork for a movie offer are growing increasingly remote.

Those who are writing for the movies get wonderful returns and the exposure causes sales and reputations to soar. Each success seems to engender further and greater success.

The Broadway theatre is the most wonderful medium of all for the song writers who write music for hit shows. Although a song writer may receive only a small advance allowance to write the music, once the show has opened and a long run is envisioned, he begins to collect on his percentage deal. The song writer of a Broadway musical usually gets 3 percent of the gross house income. Hit musicals gross in excess of $70,000 weekly. A year of such grosses would bring the song writer $110,000. Add to this his income from ASCAP (American Society of Composers and Publishers), his royalties from records and sheet music sales, and he would seem to have hit the jackpot.

Many Broadway shows are sold to the films. When this happens, the writer gets a healthy cash payment and a percentage of the movie's grosses, and so he gets back on the carousel for another go-round. Once again, there are royalties from records, sheet music, and ASCAP payments, and, adding all this to his percentage of movie receipts, it is obvious that our song writer becomes a substantial, albeit reluctant, contributor to the United States Treasury.

Often it happens that successful Broadway show composers are chosen to write songs for the motion picture industry. This is a creative task separate from transferring a Broadway show to the medium of film. Such famed musical comedy writers as George Gershwin, Richard Rodgers, Jerome Kern, Harold Arlen, Irving Berlin, and Cole Porter have all had notable movie successes.

Off Broadway shows, original night club revues, and industrial shows, while in no way rivaling the lucrative opportunities of Broadway, are excellent showcases for composers. (An industrial show, as referred to here, is an original musical show usually produced by a manufacturer. It employs original music and lyrics and either an original book of sketches. Using singers, dancers, and actors, the whole show is one giant commercial, although its theme may not necessarily dwell on the product throughout.)

Several writers have stepped up from this kind of minor-league operation into the real big time, but the most disturbing thing about the Broadway scene is that so few composers are slicing large portions out of this pie of gold, although it is understandable that people who make such enormous investments as those that are required to mount a modern musical are unwilling to entrust important roles to unknown, untried song writers. Besides, the name value of established musical comedy writers serves to bring people to the show.

The young writer is urged to write as often as possible and to spare no effort to see that his music is played, recorded, and published. Further, he should join either ASCAP or BMI (Broadcast Music, Inc.), because even at its pedestrian level of moderate success, song writing brings substantial returns, which continue all during the lives of active composers. Such returns are better than royalties and take far less investment than would be required to bring the same return from securities.

ASCAP and BMI license, on behalf of their members, the right to perform the copyrighted musical works of their members. What this means, in practice, is that through a complex system of monitoring performances, live and on radio, television etc., ASCAP and BMI receive license fees which they distribute to their members. Depending on which of the two organizations one belongs to (you may only belong to one at a time) and which plan of those they offer you choose, the composer is paid either a straight fee for each performance of his work or an annual figure based on his performances averaged over a period of time. Even a modest song writing success can result in an income of $10,000–$15,000 a year.

I would be a fool if I thought I could impart a formula or procedure for becoming a successful song writer. If I knew one, I would probably be writing Broadway shows myself. I am well acquainted with many people who write exceptionally good tunes and yet are unable to make the least impression in the field.

An inordinate amount of leg work seems to be the order of the day, not only in having a first song taken but in continuing to have succeeding tunes accepted and recorded. All of the big Tin Pan Alley names suffered disappointment and humiliation before even a first tune was published. Today, it is more difficult than ever, but those with confidence in themselves go out day after day, visiting A. and R. men, publishers, anyone at all who may be interested in a new tune. The "Nos" are as curt as ever. The insults to you and your work may be degrading. The difficulty of making appointments with recording company people will be very great, as will the number of broken engagements. Losing heart and giving up may appear to be the easiest way out, but the big names of today, despite one discouragement after another, never gave up, and, even if the world is not richer for it (and it surely must be), at least they are.

Make the rounds every day. Show more stamina than the A. and R. men have. Do not let slighting remarks wither your determination; only be sure you have something worthwhile to offer. Perhaps a chance meeting with an Off Broadway producer who is looking for a fresh approach to show tunes will give you your first assignment. At least try, try, try! Eventually someone's resistance will be worn down, and if it will happen for you at all, it will happen this way. It is most certainly worth it, and the rewards can be enormous.

CHAPTER XV

The Accompanist

Although we shall treat this area briefly, it is by no means to be considered an unimportant field. The successful performance of many an artist is not only intimately connected with, but often largely dependent upon, the quality and the taste of the accompanist. "The auxiliary role of the accompaniment frequently leads to an under-estimation of its musical and artistic importance, on the part of the soloist as well as the audience," wrote Willi Apel in the "Harvard Dictionary of Music." "Vocalists, especially, are inclined to demand an undue subordination of their accompanists, condemning them to complete slavery in question of interpretation, of tempo, of dynamics, etc. This situation is the more dangerous, since the possession of an outstanding voice and vocal technique is no guarantee of musical taste and artistic discrimination."

G. A. Briggs, the manufacturer and developer of the famous Wharfedale loudspeakers, in his informative book called "Pianos, Pianists, and Sonics" (published by Wharfedale Wireless Works), first recommends reading "The Unashamed Accompanist" by Gerald Moore, which is a serious attempt to raise the art of accompaniment to a position of stature, its rightful place. Then he writes, "The position today is that the so-called accompaniment to many songs is far more interesting than the solo, and is often more difficult to perform. Such works would have been better described as 'Duet for voice and piano.' The position is rather better with instrumental music, where a long work is called a sonata and the pianist is promoted to equal

status with the violinist or 'cellist or flautist, etc., as the case may be.
. . . A superb artist at the piano sometimes mitigates the feeling of
being soaked with sentiment by the voice which saturates the micro-
phone. I suppose that, in such cases, the crooner is paid about ten
times as much as the accompanist; the ratio of remuneration should
be reversed."

There are hundreds of pianists who derive their income from ac-
companying solo performers and, in churches, organists who accompany solo singers and choirs.

The pianist who accompanies the violin virtuoso is very much an
artist himself, and his training, therefore, is that of the concert artist.
The accompanist of a highly paid concert artist can have a long,
fruitful career, and will often stay very many years with the same
soloist. A well paid accompanist may get from $200–$300 a performance.

Women accompanists frequently cite sex discrimination, claiming
that both men and women are afraid female accompanists will take
away attention from the soloists. Accompanists of both sexes suffer
from lack of public recognition and insufficient remuneration compared to the artist they are assisting. In fact, an accompanist has no
way of knowing if his soloist is earning $500 or $5000 for a concert.
Some attempts have been made to start an organization of "assisting
artists" to establish a minimum fee, obtain information about soloists'
fees, a proportion of which the accompanist would receive over a
minimum set amount, and to establish use of signed contracts. So far,
these attempts have not met with success.

Young artists whose fees are quite small require accompanists
just as do the mature soloists who've arrived. Unable to pay large
salaries to accompanists, the better-known pianists are unavailable to
them. Young promising accompanists are offered a good deal of fine
experience as well as an opportunity to build a reputation by joining
forces with such young soloists.

In the pop field, since much that the accompanist plays is im-
provised (or at least not written out note for note), the demands on
his taste are great. Also, the accompanist who can literally breathe
with and anticipate every gesture of the artist finds his services in-

dispensable. Such accompanists frequently are called upon to arrange or conduct for their employers' acts. Often, in addition to playing the piano, they arrange *and* conduct.

While pop artists' accompanists have relatively long careers to look forward to, the length of time spent with any one artist is dependent upon the personal relationship between artist and pianist.

Salaries for accompanists of top stars tend to be much higher than for their counterparts on the concert stage. Personal and social contact, mutual friends, artists' managers, and "bookers" are the most effective agents for bringing accompanists to the attention and into the employ of artists.

CHAPTER XVI

Music Education

The job outlook in music teaching is not as optimistic in 1975 as it was, say, a decade ago due to a declining birthrate, pinched school budgets, and a trend on the college level toward larger classes and greater utilization of graduate assistants. Further exacerbating the situation are the increased numbers of qualified teachers on the job market because of the much publicized shortages predicted in the 50's and 60's.

One teacher placement agency in New York City, which places teachers all over the country at all levels, reports that music openings are very limited as of 1975. They have found that many schools have combined music with another cirriculum area, while some want only part-time music teachers (ideal for women with families). This agency further reports that most university requests have been for instrumentalists with Ph.Ds, and at the elementary level the main need is for music K-6, which often requires certification in ele-mentary education rather than music.

There are many who do not wish to engage in full-time teaching. Many of our principal symphony players are also on the faculties of the big conservatories and music schools in their localities. Many teach privately. Church organists and choirmasters find teaching provides an excellent supplement to their income.

Musicians who travel have difficulty in maintaining regular teach-ing schedules, but those who stay in one place have a variety of op-portunities to pursue. One musician of my acquaintance who plays the string bass has a regular teaching post in the public-school system. After school, he teaches privately, and on his weekends he plays club dates. In Birmingham, Alabama, I met a pianist whose private teaching practice includes one hundred students. He told me that he gives an average of eighty half-hour lessons each week. In addition, he works at a local club on weekends (Friday and Saturday) and whenever a musical event takes place or an attraction comes to Birmingham, with local musicians being employed, he gets called. Both these men make very comfortable incomes.

Those who teach instrumental playing may have difficulty finding students for some instruments. There is no dearth of pupils wishing to study piano, violin, trumpet, accordion, saxophone, clarinet, flute, or percussion. However, a shortage of string players is indicated by the unwillingness of enough students to undertake the study of viola and 'cello. Teachers of oboe, English horn, bassoon, and French horn rarely prosper except in those cities able to support well-integrated regular symphonic seasons, probably because the orchestra's presence stirs up interest in these instruments. With the increasing popularity of relatively inexpensive electric and electronic organs, teachers of that instrument are adding substantially to their rosters of students. Harp, on the other hand, being such a prohibitively expensive instrument will find fewer students than might wish to learn the instrument.

The main areas of music education include the public-school system, private schools, colleges and universities, music schools, and private instruction. The chief advantage of a position in a school as against private instruction is that a guaranteed salary is offered, one that is not dependent upon the whims of the public and their children in the community.

Further the status of educators is in the ascendancy as are their salaries. The average salary for a classroom teacher in public elementary and secondary schools for 1972–'73 was $10,100 and for '73–'74, $10,600, but teachers with only a baccalaureate and no experience can start as low as $6000. Increments are based on the number of degrees held and the number of years in the system. In New York City, for example (where salaries are higher than the

nation's average), a teacher with a B.A. receives a starting salary of
$9,700 and with a Ph.D. and all the available increments can earn
$20,350. Private schools and colleges without public funds generally
start teachers at a lower figure, but a number of colleges pay their
top people over $30,000 a year. These salaries are all on the basis of
a nine to ten month year and a teacher may, of course, pick up extra
money by teaching a summer session. The parochial school teacher
is apt to earn from $5,500 to $13,500.

The requirements for teaching in the public schools vary from
state to state and many require the M.A. or its equivalent in graduate
courses for permanent certification. If the degree conferred was not
taken in education, additional study leading to a teacher's certificate
is mandatory in most states. In New York State, for example, the
requirements for permanent certification teaching music are as follows: baccalaureate including thirty-six semester hours of music,
twelve semester hours of education courses plus student teaching,
master's degree in or related to field of teaching or thirty semester
hours of graduate study distributed among social and behavioral
sciences, music, and professional study in education. To receive a
permanent music supervisor's certificate, added to this is: completion
of program for preparation of administrators and supervisors or
thirty semester hours of graduate study including eighteen hours of
graduate study in or related to fields of education administration and
supervision; supervisory internship under supervision of practicing
school administrator; three years of approved teaching and/or administrative and/or supervisory experience. Of course, the supervisor
earns more than the classroom teacher.

In all public schools in America the "step" system of advancement
is practiced. The number of steps varies from system to system and
in New York City it consists of sixteen semi-annual steps which
means a teacher reaches maximum pay after eight years. Differentials
are based on the number of degrees held.

Most schools have pension plans for teachers and among them that
of New York City is noteworthy. After twenty years in the system,
the teacher retires at half pay. Public schools give tenure. That is,
after three years of teaching, in most systems, tenure is granted and

the teacher may be dismissed only for "due cause." Unfortunately, this phrase does not only apply to incompetence, alcoholism or the like, but such unavoidable contingencies as school budget cuts. The music teacher, often considered only a "frill," can lose a job in such a situation. Most schools give sabbaticals after extended service. This is a leave at partial pay for projects which will improve the teacher's performance upon his return.

Public-school music teachers have a variety of duties, any of which they may be called upon to perform. Directing singing classes, choirs, bands, and orchestras are the chief duties. Some instructors are required to teach a number of instruments to members of orchestras and bands. Music appreciation is frequently taught, but only rarely are courses in history, solfeggio, or theory taught. Frequently, music teachers are required to teach other subjects—or, more accurately, teachers of other subjects are frequently required to teach music.

Enterprising teachers should not be discouraged from deviating from the prescribed syllabus to offer some knowledge of music theory, or to arrange and compose for groups with which they work. Class work in ear training, sight reading, dictation, and counting can be a valuable adjunct to music appreciation, for it stimulates the student's perception of musical shapes and forms. Even occasional attempts at creative writing whet a group's interest in music.

Many teachers of music who work in the public-school system are very happy in their careers. They enjoy being challenged by alert children and feel a tremendous sense of accomplishment at seeing youngsters progress. These teachers love the life, which they find so serene when compared with the hurly-burly in other fields of music. This is especially true of teachers who have come from the field of performing to the world of education.

Private-school teaching is largely similar to that of the public schools. The main differences are that the teaching certificate may not be required, although the M.A. is more often required than in public school. Also, there is apt to be a lower starting salary, and security in the position may not be equal to that of the public-school teacher. Pension plans, also, are less apt to be as good as in the public schools. On the other hand, top salaries at some of the better private schools may exceed anything the public-school teacher could reasonably anticipate.

At the college level it's expected that the instructor hold at least a master's. According to an American Council on Education Research Report for 1972–73, only five percent of those on college faculties (for all fields) held only a B.A. Those wishing to teach at our best colleges and universities should hold a doctorate, and it is desirable to secure a position at even the less well-known schools. The proportion of Ph.Ds on the faculties of two year (junior) colleges is somewhat lower than for regular four year schools.

It is frequently necessary (particularly in smaller schools) for the music teacher to carry courses outside his specialty. Someone with a Ph.D. in musicology may be required to teach theory or an instrument as well. An instrumentalist, on the other hand, should have considerable mastery of the theoretical subjects (harmony, counterpoint, fugue, orchestration, composition) as well as a far-reaching knowledge of music history. If he plans to teach electronic music, he should have more than elementary knowledge of electronics.

It is to be hoped that the music teacher will have the opportunity to teach according to his special abilities or in his special field of interest, but such is not necessarily always the case. Since teachers are assigned courses according to the needs of the school's curriculum and the abilities of the rest of its staff, the potential music teacher is encouraged to be as widely versed as possible. Present-day thinking tends to give much weight to the idea that a knowledge of the arts is basic to an understanding of music. Such knowledge is desirable and it is usually expected.

The School of Music at one of our top universities pays its faculty salaries ranging from $9,400 to $31,200. This same school reports that its recent graduates have taken initial salaries ranging from $8,000 to $15,000. But, remember, this is one of the top schools. Other graduates must settle for considerably less, and there is no doubt that a certain number of qualified music teachers are underemployed or forced to take non-music positions.

Tables on average salaries for college teachers indicates a steady increase which is expected to continue. For 1972–73 these average figures were as follows: universities, $15,869; other four year institutions, $13,493; two year colleges, $12,890. These salaries are for men. Those for women are somewhat lower, and studies do indicate that women are still frequently paid less than men in the same positions with equivalent qualifications. However, it should also be noted that the disparity also represents the fact that men are better prepared than their female counterparts; 33.8 percent of men on college faculties hold Ph.Ds compared with 15.6 percent of women. (Wives more frequently support their husband through graduate school than the other way around.)

One other practice at the university level is becoming increasingly widespread. This is the tendency to employ resident musicians. There are resident string quartets, resident wood-wind groups, and resident mixed chamber ensembles. Musicians who go into residency must be outstanding instrumentalists, although no degree is required. Such men are usually given an associate degree in music and are considered part of the faculty. Their duties are to give chamber music concerts, teach chamber music and its playing, and occasionally take part in university musical events. Some may be asked to conduct or, if they have the skills, to teach a course or two in theory.

At the college level, the rewards are regular if not inordinately high. Only in the early years of university teaching is there insecurity. After each of the first two years, the instructor is either hired for another year or dropped. Only after three years, in most colleges, is tenure granted. From then on, much of the pressure is off.

Appointment to a teaching post at the college level or in public or private schools usually requires first sending a résumé together with a letter asking for a position. They should be sent to superintendents, principals, faculty personnel offices, or to teacher agencies that specialize (for a fee) in securing positions for qualified teachers. The résumé should contain the applicant's age, marital status, education, instrument played, professional musical experience, teaching experience, and scholastic honors, if any.

The big conservatories that confer music degrees are divided into two parts. Although their principal aims are to develop well-rounded musicians, the emphasis tends to be on performance. The better schools are equipped to prepare virtuoso performers for concert careers, and a major in conducting or composition can bring great proficiency. That constitutes one part. The other department of the better conservatories has a faculty of teachers who give instruction in theory and history.

The instrumental teachers are sought out by the conservatory and offered positions. It is no surprise that many of them go back to teach at the conservatory from which they were graduated. Often they are members of the local symphony orchestra, usually occupying key chairs. The most common arrangement involves no salary to the instrumental teacher. He lends his prestige to the conservatory. The conservatory gives the teacher its prestige. The teacher uses the facilities of the conservatory and is allowed to have a studio there, and in exchange teaches students enrolled at the conservatory. The students often have a choice of teachers when more than one teaches the same instrument. Sometimes, however, the teacher exercises his choice. Frequently, the teacher is allowed to set his own price. In some instances, he may keep all the money that comes to him from this source. In other cases, he may have to give a small fee for each student to the conservatory.

The other half of the faculty, which teaches theory and history, is hired and paid in similar fashion to university teachers. Degrees from conservatories or colleges are usually required and the salary is often based upon the repute of the teacher. Some schools give tenure; others do not.

The small private music school is a combination of private teaching with a business enterprise. It is usually not profitable to teach in such a school. The owner or owners alone are able to derive sufficient profit from such an undertaking. Instruction in instrumental playing is given almost exclusively. I have never heard of such a private venture teaching theory or history. Occasionally, arranging is taught, but most of the teachers in schools of this sort could not teach theory or history even if they felt they should.

The lessons cost from $4 up to $6 for half an hour of elementary or intermediate instruction. Advanced instruction frequently costs more. The teacher has to give the school from 25 to 40 percent of his take. Out of the percentage received from the teacher, the owner has to maintain the studios, pay for publicity, recitals, and new equipment. If he has a secretary, he pays her salary, too. The owner or owners may often take some students themselves.

Many such schools have dealer-type agreements with instrument manufacturers. Thus, any instrument sold produces a profit for the school and a commission for the teacher.

The vast majority of schools of this kind have incompetent instructors who are musically illiterate and unable to teach anything beyond the most rudimentary steps. That some of their students occasionally gain proficiency is a tribute to the talent and tenacity of the students. Many of these schools care little about the progress of the students; the owners unscrupulously see to it that students play a new song from time to time just to please the mothers and fathers and so keep the money coming in.

This situation does not exist in the few good private schools that one finds in various cities. Some are staffed with competent teachers, many of them virtuosos. The owners of such schools are artists in their own right—sincere, conscientious scholars who are anxious to see that the musical talents of their students are carefully nurtured. Many such owners are university and conservatory graduates, and a number of them have gone back to school to gain a surer knowledge of teaching methods and psychology.

A number of private music schools have opened branches in other cities, and some have grown into chain-store operations. As stated earlier, some chain-school organizations, at the national level, are sizable businesses and bring big profits to their owners. However, my feelings toward this kind of a music school are similar to what they would be toward my physician if he suddenly opened offices, in a chain-like manner, all over the country.

One remaining field of teaching should be remarked upon. This is the field of private instruction. Although it is admittedly difficult for teachers of several different instruments to establish a thriving practice, some instruments lend themselves admirably to satisfying the needs and wants of a community. I would never suppose that a tuba teacher would find his studio swamped with students, but the list of instruments mentioned earlier are taught successfully and profitably by many, many teachers in many lands. Piano and violin traditionally lead the list, with piano probably at the top.

Although most teachers earn only about $5 for thirty minutes, many teachers habitually charge $12 for a half-hour lesson, and their time is so filled that they have long waiting lists. A great many teachers give hour lessons and charge from $25–$40 per lesson.

Some teachers teach theory along with the lesson, but this is impractical in half-hour periods. At least forty minutes is needed for a lesson if theory is to be taught at all.

The private teacher who is able to build up a large practice should be able to earn from $15,000 to $25,000 each year if he is conscientious, patient and skillful in his work. Private teaching can be particularly rewarding for the woman who wants to combine a career with homemaking. She can work at home part-time and gradually increase the number of hours she teaches as her children reach school age. The big disadvantage to such a woman, of course, is that her school-age pupils will only be available at the same hours as her own children are at home.

Though far from perfect, the field of teaching unquestionably deserves consideration when a career in music is contemplated. Security is higher, income is steadier, long careers are practically assured in education. Salaries are not spectacular, but at least summers are free if desired.

CHAPTER XVII

In Conclusion

Before closing, I should like to note that I am indebted to many musicians, union officials, orchestra managers, and publicity people from coast to coast for the liberal help they have given me in gathering data and salary schedules. There may be errors, but I seriously doubt if the figures given are in gross error. To have set forth the specific incomes of many people would have been an impossibility in some instances and an invasion of privacy in others.

Space has not permitted an exploration of the vitally important area that concerns singers, whose role in music is a large one. Another whole volume could easily have been devoted to their careers, which parallel those of instrumentalists in so many areas. Their problems may differ from instrumentalists, but mainly in degree. On the whole, singers earn more than instrumentalists, but in some areas, notably the Broadway theatre and the opera, those in subsidiary roles are enormously underpaid. Countering this is the large percentage of singers who become celebrities. Celebrities can and do earn fantastic amounts of money.

In planning a career in music one may also consider a number of related fields, some of which combine musical expertise with other interests. These include careers in the music "business" such as merchandising instruments, records, scores, and books. Some with mechanical abilities have established careers making or rebuilding pianos and harpsichords or being a tuner or technician. A career in law could concentrate on music related legal services like copyright law. Arts management (impressarios, artists' agents) is a specialized field requiring knowledge of business and law as well as music. Music critics, writers, and historians must be both musicians and writers. With an increase in international cultural exchange programs, jobs have opened in arts programs with foundations and government information services. A music librarian, who must have training in library science, can work in a college or university library, public library, for a TV or radio station, or an orchestra or band. The field of church music can range from being a part-time organist in a church or synagogue to being a minister of music for a large institution. Music therapy is a relatively new field involving medical knowledge and psychology. Newest of all, perhaps, is ethnomusicology, which uses music as a tool for analyzing a society using the principles of social science as well as music.

It is to be hoped that this book, despite its many shortcomings, will have done more than cause a slight rise in the profits of the office supplies company that sold me, at inflated prices, so much typing paper, carbon paper, yellow-lined pads of paper, and ball-point pen refills. It is my hope that some light has been thrown on the kinds of careers music offers, on what training and talent are necessary, and on the kind of economic status that music careers can offer.

Ira Gershwin once wrote a song called "Don't Be a Woman If You Can." If I have seemed to be saying "Don't Be a Musician If You Can," it was merely my faltering manner of demonstrating the limited scope of the opportunities, while pointing up the immense success that has come to some in these fields. If the picture is a discouraging one to some, it may be well if they decide to enter other more stable fields. Those who will not be discouraged and whose lives will be shattered by not becoming professional musicians will come into the field anyway. It is best if they know that success is not automatically a result of talent, that disappointment, hardship, and insecurity are not uncommon, that recognition may never come. It is not enough to know that the rewards for recognition can be gigantic.

That music education offers the most dependable and secure music career is of vast importance to the whole future of music. That music education is growing is the best sign of all, provided nothing stops this growth before it reaches out to touch everyone. It is not that we need more and better professional musicians to swell the ranks of the distressed. We will always have many fine professionals. The dedicated and the talented will always seek artistic fulfillment, regardless of the cost. No, it is not for them that music education is so important. It is for everyone, so we will have, in our great land, more and better amateurs, amateurs of taste and discrimination, amateurs who make of music the social experience it should be. Good amateurs playing together or for others do more to keep the interest in music alive and to broaden and improve the tastes of their fellows than all the stereo equipment there is.

The public knows that culture is expensive. It is expensive because men create it—men of extraordinary talent and training—and men cost money. In the case of our large orchestras, no mere box office receipts can carry the burden of the orchestra's expense. There is not enough interest in chamber concerts or in lesser-known artists to provide satisfactory careers for more than a few, and this is a question of economics. It takes money to support the lesser groups as well as the larger ones—lots of money.

This culture that is so expensive is everybody's business. Our concern should not be for what other countries might think of us, although shame is a powerful incentive for taking action that otherwise might be avoided. The real concern should be for providing ourselves and our children with opportunities for enrichment. Culture gives us this enrichment and education gives an understanding of culture. If appreciation of culture were universal, concern for its survival would be universal and millions would be anxious to share its burdens. At the national level each man's share of the burden is proportionately reduced.

That music is universally loved is undisputed. People created and loved music from earliest times. Music, which is as natural to mankind as eating and sleeping, will always be loved and survive any conditions, so long as man himself survives. However, only an elementary kind of music is universally loved; only an elementary kind of music pours forth from or delights the uncultivated man. No tutoring, no training, no education is required to love to sing or whistle simple tunes.

Such is not the case with most art music. Gifted composers conceived music of increasing complexity. This music did not always gush forth as water from a spring. Composers summoned all their intellectual resources to help weave the threads of their invention into coherent, logically developing, and well-balanced wholes. This is no background music intended to accompany idle pastimes. Such music demands active participation in the form of concentrated attention if one is to avoid being swamped in a sea of sound. Only the cultivated listener whose musical background has taught him to hear as he listens can comprehend such music. To all others, great music can be little more than an occasional familiar melody surrounded by long series of amorphous fragments and colors.

Boston's beloved orchestra enjoys a gallery of devoted subscribers. Friday afternoons most of the downstairs is occupied by women. Some years ago, while Serge Koussevitzky was still alive, a few of "Boston's best" began the discourteous practice of knitting throughout the concert. Following the example set by these pace-setters, more women each week took their knitting baskets to Symphony Hall until finally the audience looked more like a knitting class than a group of wealthy patrons of the arts—"music lovers." It must have been a fascinating thing for the musicians, looking out of the corners of their eyes, to see a thousand women moving their needles in concert like some form of otherworld mechanized monster—knit, purl, knit, purl. The audience noise rose to such a level that to have continued with the concert would have been absurd; the distraction could no longer be tolerated. In frustration, Dr. Koussevitzky stopped the orchestra, set his baton on his music rack, turned around and simply stared out at the audience until, slowly, the click-clack, click-clack subsided.

The women who perpetrated this graceless folly meant no offense to the orchestra, conductor, or music. They were simply incapable of understanding or appreciating the music that was performed each week at their subscription concerts. Unable to listen intelligently and thus, to hear, they were restless. Since the pose of music lover had to be maintained, the concerts had to be attended. What could it hurt if they did a little knitting to relieve the monotony?

These women only condemned themselves by their action and revealed the weakness of their musical background and education. The inability to "hear" is understandable in uncultivated listeners, but the inability of music lovers to listen intelligently is profoundly disturbing. It was tragic that Beethoven, although he retained his keen inner hearing, lost his outer physical hearing, but it is a greater tragedy that so many people whose ears are completely normal lack so completely the ability to listen and to grasp what they hear.

Music is the most natural and least artificial as well as the most complicated and subtle of all the arts. Of course, anyone can derive a good deal of pleasure from putting himself in contact with music, by opening his ears and letting an infinite variety of colors and rhythms engulf him. Unfortunately, too many people whose pleasure in music stems from the sensuous quality of its sound are satisfied to let it go at that; they already enjoy music so why expend the effort to gain a mature appreciation?

If music education grows as it should in coming years, it will become an important part of the curriculum in all elementary and secondary schools. A well-planned, well-integrated program for teaching music through the twelve grades, especially if conducted by competent instructors, will develop an appreciation for, and skills in, a medium of expression for which all young people have a natural aptitude and affinity.

Music has no other access to the person than through the ear. We are all endowed with this remarkable sense, the sense of hearing. What a pity it is not to develop it, to prevent ourselves from sharing the joys of music. If in an extended music course children's ears are trained, if their minds are disciplined to sort the multitude of sounds that strike the tympanum, to retain and recognize musical details— in short, to "hear" tonal relationships—the major problem of music appreciation by the masses will have been conquered. It is not as difficult as it appears; it merely takes a well-directed, consistent effort applied for an extended period of time. If such a program were adopted, our high schools would be filled with young people whose discriminating ears would put their parents to shame. We would be blessed with high school graduates whose awareness of the language of music would prompt them upon hearing a work for the first time, to ask themselves not, "Do I like it?" but "Do I understand it?"

Lack of general music education for the masses explains the lack of true appreciation on the part of so many in this country. A far-reaching program for music education would, in time, create an atmosphere of sympathy to music and a desire to make music as much a part of the American way of life as it is in many European countries. An awakening love of music would necessarily bring with it a love for our orchestras and artists, as well as an awareness of the problems that threaten to drive them from the field of music. A realization of the deep-seated need of Americans for their cultural institutions and for the men who contribute so much to their glory, coupled with the knowledge of the precarious economic existence that confronts American artists and composers, could have no other effect than to cause our people to take immediate steps to guarantee the survival and productivity of our artists. Yes, you do have a future in music, if music has a future in you.